# INTRODU

This prayer booklet has been a labor of love, by many people, over the span of two years.

I suppose it had its genesis in my mind as a much more scaled down, local version of Patrick Johnstone's *Operation World*;[1] a sort of Chicago-focused edition of WayMakers *Seek God for the City*.[2] In many ways, YWAMer Brad Stanley helped us initially zero in on praying for the nations in our city a few years ago.[3]

Pastor Jackson Crum of Park Community Church initially sparked my interest reminding our staff and congregation of the 221 micro-neighborhoods within the 77 communities of Chicago in the context of seeking the shalom, or just peace, of the city and praying to the Lord on its behalf (Jeremiah 29:7).

And so we tasked an intern from Wheaton College, Mackenzie Magnus, to start the process. She handed her work over to Talia Cork at Park, and I in turn, entrusted her work to an undergrad group of Moody students, as a class project for Understanding the City.

Next, a number of grad students at Moody continued to chip away at it in my Evangelism and Community Analysis course, most notably Matt Johnson, under the watchful eyes of my project manager, Elizabeth Koenig, and a Northwestern alum Grace Lyu. Another Park young woman contributed her efforts in the early stages as well, Sarah Abbey. But Elizabeth and Grace especially gave countless hours, and with Matt's 11th hour assistance, the four of us together finally wrestled it to completion.

Thanks as well to Rachel Quanstrom, Josh Burns, and Brittany VanErem, colleagues at Park, for your help with format, layout, printing, and cover design. Couldn't have done it without you guys!

We were informed by the holistic nature of Psalm 122:6–8 to pray for the shalom of our city, with specific criteria in mind:

1) Spiritual vitality: 6a
2) Economic health: 6b
3) Physical safety: 7a
4) Political justice: 7b
5) Social relationships: 8

# INTRODUCTION

There is much biblical material that informs our prayers. We referenced part of that framework and instilled it into the context of this prayer guide. The four categories referenced are: God's heart for the city; the widow, orphan, stranger, and poor; justice goodness, and compassion; and prayer and unity. Verses from these categories were chosen and assigned for each neighborhood.

We are also keenly aware that while we were hard at work on this guide, over five hundred young people were shot and killed in many of the more marginalized communities of Chicago this past year. And in the first six months of this year in our city, there have been one thousand shootings. We feel a bit like Queen Esther, in chapter 8:6, "...how can I endure to see the calamity which shall befall my people..."

The words of 2 Chronicles 7:14 certainly still apply: "If my people, who are called by my name, humble themselves and pray, and seek my face, and turn from their wicked ways, then I will hear from heaven, will forgive their sin, and will heal their land."

To that end, we offer up this guide. We know that our great God loves Chicago and its people, and we sincerely believe that by encouraging the broader body of Christ in Chicago to pray, He will break our hearts for each and every one of our neighborhoods with a renewed love and compassion and conviction to "engage in good deeds" (Titus 3:14).

It is also our hope that this *Chicago Neighborhood Prayer Guide* could rally a similar prayer focus across other cities in our nation and around the world. May God give us tears for our cities.

Dr. John Fuder
Resource Global | docfuder@resourceglobal.org
Heart for the City | www.h4tc.org
Chicago, IL
October 2013

1 Patrick Johnstone, *Operation World: The Day-by-Day Guide to Praying For the World.* (Grand Rapids: Zondervan, 1993).
2 WayMakers, *Seek God for the City 2013.* (Austin: WayMakers, 2013).
3 *Ethnic Embrace Chicago: a 31-day prayer guide.* (Chicago: GlobalROAR, 2009).

# ALBANY PARK

**PSALM 9:9**

*The Lord will be a stronghold for the oppressed . . .
in times of trouble.*

## NEIGHBORHOODS

Albany Park, Mayfair, North Mayfair, Ravenswood Manor

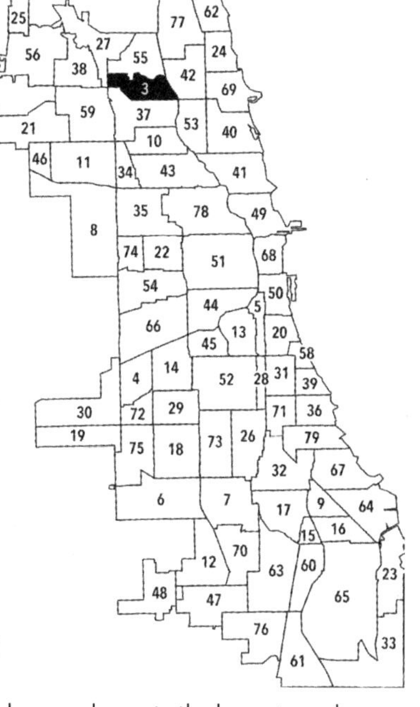


## DEMOGRAPHICS

Asian (12.7%), Black or African American (4.3%), Hispanic or Latino (51.0%), White (30.2%)

## LEARN

Annexed to Chicago in 1893, Albany Park is now home to one of the most ethnically diverse zip codes in the country. Initially settled by German and Swedish immigrants, Albany Park became home to a number of Russian Jews after 1912. Following World War II, many Jewish families moved north, leaving Albany Park during the economic and social decline. The population dropped drastically as homes and stores became vacant, leading to the development of illegal drug trade, prostitution, and gangs. In response, city government and other corporations worked to improve Albany Park through streetscape development, low-interest loans, and financing packages. These efforts brought a return of residents and an increase in property values. In 1990, Albany Park became home to the largest number of Korean, Filipino, and Guatemalan immigrants in Chicago and became known as the "Ellis Island" of Chicago. The population continues to shift as Korean immigrants move to northern suburbs.[1]

## PRAY

As one of the most ethnically diverse neighborhoods in Chicago, Albany Park is a community of many religions. Pray for truth to reign in the hearts of the people and the gospel to break through cultural boundaries and strongholds.

There are several churches and organizations that are working with the refugee population. Pray that God would give them favor and the necessary resources to serve the refugees.

Many churches have been recently planted to address the diversity in this neighborhood. Pray that their efforts would take root in the lives of the community residents.

Pray for those that are marginalized in this community, such as the homeless and undocumented residents. Pray that they may reestablish connectedness to family, employment, and schooling.

1 Neary, Timothy B. Albany Park. Encyclopedia of Chicago. http://encyclopedia.chicagohistory.org/pages/36.html.

# ARCHER HEIGHTS

**REV. 21:2–4**

*. . . the new Jerusalem . . . God shall be among them . . .*
*there shall no longer be any death . . .*

## NEIGHBORHOODS

Archer Heights

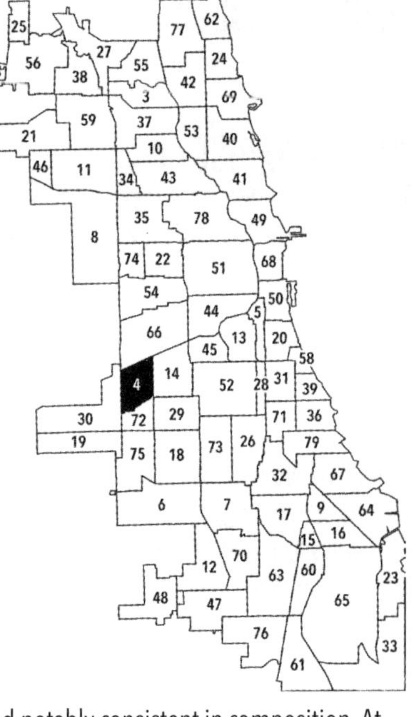


## DEMOGRAPHICS

Asian (0%), Black or African American (1.4%), Hispanic or Latino (67.8%), White (30.1%)

## LEARN

During the 1850s, Archer Heights remained undeveloped swampland, home to few settlers. There was little economic development in the area despite the establishment of the Illinois & Michigan Canal, the Chicago & Alton Railroad, and Archer Road. After the turn of the century in 1900, spectators developed residential sections of Archer Heights. The establishment of electric streetcars by 1906 created an influx of Poles, Italians, Lithuanians, Czechs, and Russian Jews. The 1930s and 1940s brought industrial and commercial growth and about two-thirds of the area became industry. Residential growth, however, picked up again following World War II. The population fluctuated between 1950 and 1990 with the decline of Midway's significance as the main airport in Chicago. During this time, the population remained notably consistent in composition. At the end of the twentieth century, 60 percent of Archer Heights was for manufacturing and bulk transportation facilities, 30 percent was residential, and 10 percent was commercial. The character of Archer Heights remained consistent throughout the twentieth century as a mostly blue-collar, Caucasian, and industrial population. In the early twenty-first century, the population began to shift as a large number of Hispanic families moved into the neighborhood.[1]

## PRAY

As the social landscape of this neighborhood changes rapidly, the residents are experiencing racial and language barriers. Pray for churches to come alongside the people and help alleviate the tensions.

There are many families that have been displaced and fragmented in this community. Pray for stability and that they would discover their belonging as members of the family of God.

Pray for young people to stay in school and stem the tide of high dropout rates in this community. Pray for teachers and administrators to persevere and inspire students to see the value of education.

1 Keyes, Jonathan J. Archer Heights. Encyclopedia of Chicago. http://encyclopedia.chicagohistory.org/pages/60.html.

# ARMOUR SQUARE

**PROVERBS 14:31B**

*He who is gracious to the needy honors Him.*

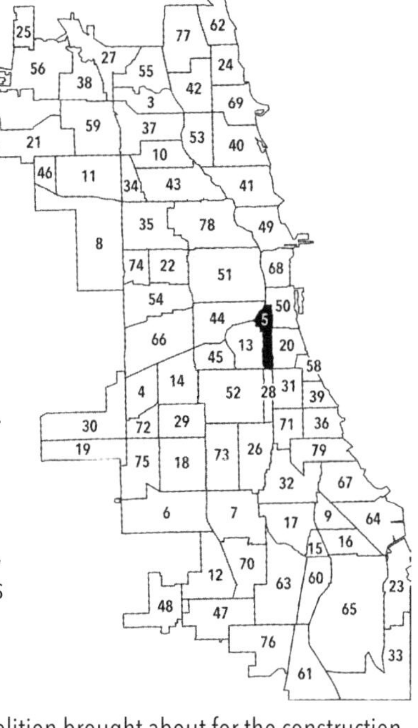


## NEIGHBORHOODS

Armour Square, Chinatown, Wentworth Gardens

## DEMOGRAPHICS

Asian (67.9%), Black or African American (9.1%), Hispanic or Latino (3.7%), White (16.5%)

## LEARN

Armour Square found its beginnings when German, Irish, and Swedish immigrants arrived during the Civil War. Around 1912, Chinese living on the south edge of the Loop began a mass movement southward, encountering severe racial discrimination. They were forced to do business through an intermediary. The H.O. Stone Company acted on behalf of fifty Chinese businessmen, securing leases on buildings in what has since become a major tourist attraction in Chicago. During World War I, the narrow corridor that was limited to African American residents on Chicago's South Side, known as the "Black Belt," expanded into the southern section of Armour Square. Chicago Housing Authority's construction of Wentworth Gardens in 1947 brought the population in the area to an all-time high. However, the demolition brought about for the construction of the Dan Ryan and Stevenson Expressway resulted in a steady decline in population. The distinctive Chinatown and Wentworth Gardens has made Armour Square the diverse environment it is today.[1]

## PRAY

Pray for the long-term development of the community as a new generation of leaders are taking over and starting to emerge.

Many immigrants are mainland Chinese students coming to America specifically for an education, which provides a window of opportunity to share the gospel with these students during their short time here.

Praise God for the work He is doing through a number of Christian social service agencies and churches in the community that provide ESL services, job training, and tutoring classes.

Recently, Chinatown businesses have gained the interest of foreign investors, with new and different understanding of business than the traditional. Pray that tensions among people in business would be mediated and resolved.

Pray that the underground issues and tensions, especially trafficking, would be addressed and not tolerated by the community.

1 Solzman, David M. Armour Square. Encyclopedia of Chicago. http://encyclopedia.chicagohistory.org/pages/71.html.

# ASHBURN

**TITUS 3:14**

*And let our people also learn to engage in good deeds to meet pressing needs . . .*

## NEIGHBORHOODS

Ashburn, Ashburn Estates, Beverly View, Crestline, Parkview, Scottsdale, Wrightwood

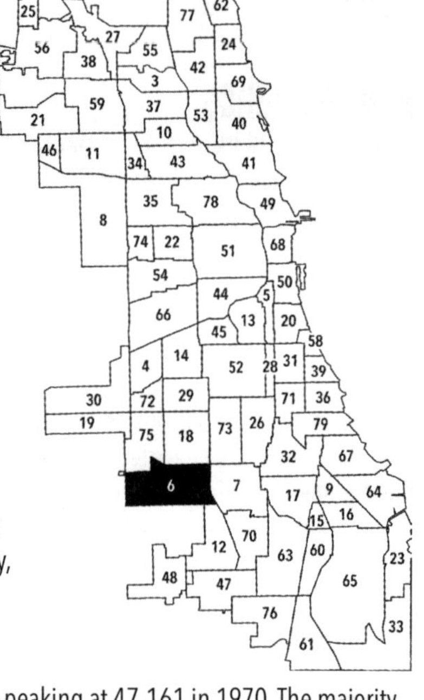


## DEMOGRAPHICS

Asian (0.8%), Black or African American (49.2%), Hispanic or Latino (31.5%), White (17.6%)

## LEARN

Following Ashburn's annexation to Chicago in 1893, railroads were built in hopes that the community would flourish. However, Ashburn was slow in development, and by 1894, only a few homes and residences were added. Chicago's first airport, Ashburn Flying Field, was opened in 1916, which became a training camp for Signal Corps during World War I. By this time, Ashburn's population had grown to 1,363. The Municipal Airport (now Midway) then opened in 1927 in a neighboring community, and Ashburn Field closed in 1939, later becoming a suburban-style mall. Although the population of Ashburn shrank down to 731 during World War II, the automobile and post-WWII baby boom led to rapid growth in the community, with the population peaking at 47,161 in 1970. The majority of the population was white until a new racially mixed neighborhood, Maycrest, formed. During the 1960s, neighborhoods integrated with the help of Greater Ashburn Planning Association (GAPA), which worked to minimize racial strife over school desegregation. Ashburn has maintained an extremely high homeownership rate, with retirement housing to help families age in the same place.[1]

## PRAY

Praise God for the ethnic diversity in the community. Pray for cultural sensitivity and continued peace among the residents.

Pray for the local high school which, though underresourced, brings together young people from many socioeconomic backgrounds.

Praise God that this community has not experienced the instances of violence and gang activity of neighboring communities. Pray that these patterns of safety would continue in Ashburn. A once vibrant church presence has waned in recent years. Pray for a renewed focus on the part of the body of Christ.

1 Meyer, Sherry. Ashburn. Encyclopedia of Chicago. http://encyclopedia.chicagohistory.org/pages/85.html.

# AUBURN GRESHAM

**PHILIPPIANS 1:4**

*. . . always offering prayer with joy in my every*

## NEIGHBORHOODS

Auburn Gresham, Gresham

## DEMOGRAPHICS

Asian (0.1%), Black or African American (98.3%), Hispanic or Latino (0.7%), White (0.4%)

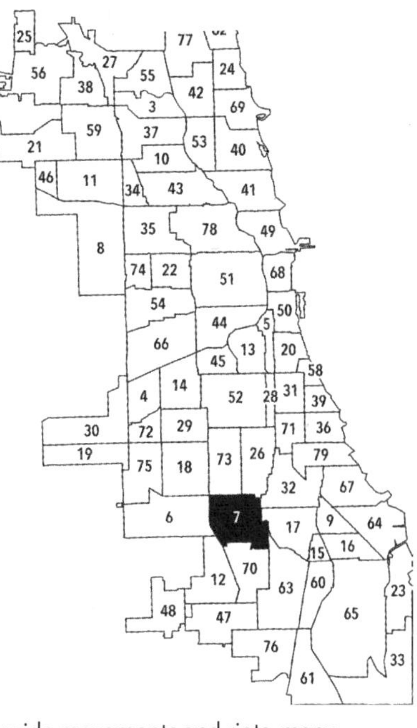


## LEARN

Auburn Gresham was annexed to Chicago in 1889 comprising German and Dutch settlers. Later, Irish settlers moved to the area and grew to 21 percent of the population. Near the end of the 1950s, African Americans began leaving the overcrowded corridor on Chicago's South Side referred to as the "Black Belt" and moved into the neighborhoods surrounding Auburn Gresham. To address the developing racial tensions, churches and civic organizations formed the Organization of Southwest Communities (OSC) in 1959. Their goal was to implement stable racial integration by maintaining property values, eliminating racist stereotypes, and preventing violence. However, in the 1960s, crime grew at a fast pace. Simultaneously, the population of Auburn Gresham increased dramatically. With national and citywide movements and riots, many white residents left the region. By 1970, Auburn Gresham was settled by a 69 percent African American population. While the OSC was unsuccessful in maintaining integration, the transition from a majority white to a majority black population was more peaceful than might have been otherwise.[1]

## PRAY

Pray for increased educational opportunities for children and teenagers.

Pray for the body of Christ in this community to be empowered in the gospel to provide an example for the neighborhood.

Pray for parents in this community to become more involved in the lives of their children.

Pray for a break in the poverty, violence, and crime prevalent in the neighborhood.

1 McMahon, Eileen M. Auburn Gresham. Encyclopedia of Chicago. http://encyclopedia.chicagohistory.org/pages/88.html.

# AUSTIN

**LUKE 19:41**

*He saw the city and wept over it.*

## NEIGHBORHOODS

Austin, Galewood, The Island

## DEMOGRAPHICS

Asian (0.4%), Black or African American (84.7%), Hispanic or Latino (8.3%), White (5.9%)

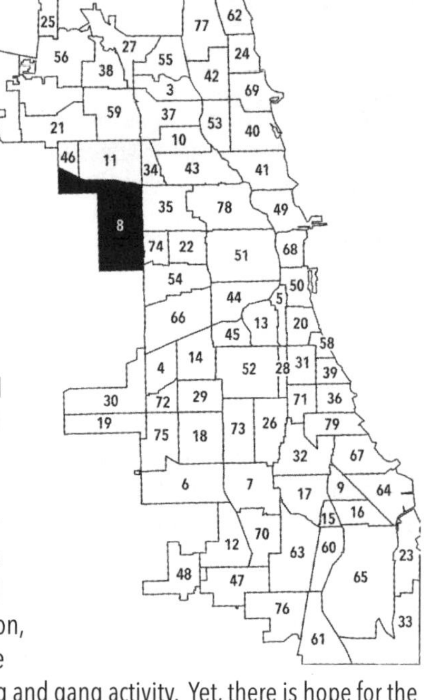


## LEARN

Henry Austin purchased 470 acres in 1865 for a temperance settlement named "Austinville" in which home ownership, tree-lined parkways, and gracious living would be the status quo. By 1920, Austin had become one of Chicago's best-served commuter neighborhoods. Germans, Scandinavians, Irish, and Italian families settled and built churches and homes, but fled during the 1960s when the demographics began to change dramatically. By 1980, Austin's population was predominantly African American. Like many other West Side communities, the neighborhood experienced the tragedy of systemic racism and white flight through housing disinvestment, vacancy, demolition, and the loss of jobs and commerce. It is currently known as one of Chicago's roughest neighborhoods, stricken with illegal drug and gang activity. Yet, there is hope for the future as Austin experiences signs of recovery through neighborhood churches and organizations.[1]

## PRAY

Pray against violence in the community, which has seen an increase in recent years due to domestic violence, drugs, gang activity, and school closures. In fact, Austin has become known as one of Chicago's most dangerous neighborhoods.

Pray for the many single-parent families, especially the struggles many women face who are left raising families by themselves. Pray for a stronger commitment to family.

In 2013, the Chicago Public School System started closing down almost fifty schools in Chicago. Several of these schools are in Austin. Pray for stability within the community during this time of transition in the school system.

Pray for the various churches in Austin to reach out to the community by getting involved in people's lives by addressing both physical and spiritual needs.

1 Martin, Judith A. Austin.Encyclopedia of Chicago. http://encyclopedia.chicagohistory.org/pages/93.html.

# AVALON PARK

**LUKE 24:49**

*. . . stay in the city until you are clothed with power from on high.*

## NEIGHBORHOODS

Avalon Park, Marynook, Stony Island Park

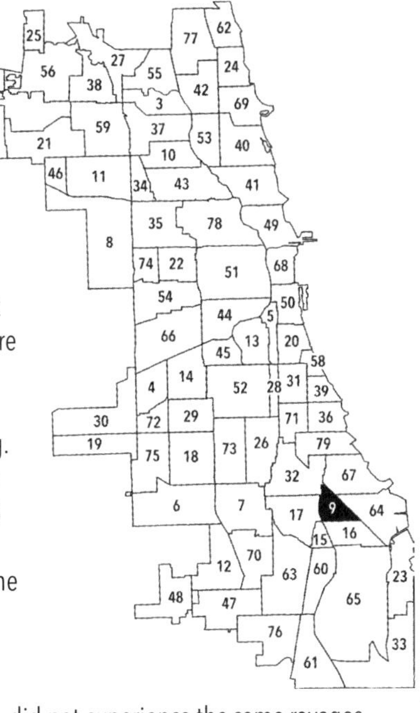


## DEMOGRAPHICS

Asian (0.3%), Black or African American (98.1%), Hispanic or Latino (0%), White (0.4%)

## LEARN

One of the unique attributes of Avalon Park are the swamps that used to occupy this territory. To avoid flooding, many houses were built on stilts during early settlement. Swamp conditions also discouraged attempts at permanent settlement, causing Avalon Park to serve as a site for waste disposal rather than family living. By the 1880s, German and Irish descendants began to reside in the community. Also, the World's Columbian Exposition of 1893 and the installation of drainage in 1900 stimulated residential growth. Then, in 1910, the former "Pennytown" changed its name officially to Avalon Park. The 1920s brought a second housing boom of single-family brick bungalows and a few apartments. African Americans began to move into Avalon Park during the 1960s and made up 96 percent of the population by 1980. They did not experience the same ravages white flight usually brought, enabling owner-occupancy rates to remain consistently over 70 percent in recent decades.[1]

## PRAY

The Nation of Islam has a strong presence in the broader community in Avalon Park. Pray for young African American men to discover their true identity in Christ.

Numerous businesses in the neighborhood are struggling, making the availability of local job opportunities scarce for the residents. Pray for economic renewal of the community.

Like many other neighborhoods in Chicago, the community is a "food desert" with a lack of fresh fruits and vegetables for families resulting in an improper diet and health concerns. Pray for initiatives to educate residents in healthy eating patterns and for affordable alternatives.

1 Best, Wallace. Avalon Park. Encyclopedia of Chicago. http://encyclopedia.chicagohistory.org/pages/97.html.

# AVONDALE

**JEREMIAH 24:7**

*Seek the welfare of the city . . . pray to the Lord on its behalf . . .*

## NEIGHBORHOODS

Avondale, Jackowo, The Polish Village, Waclowowo

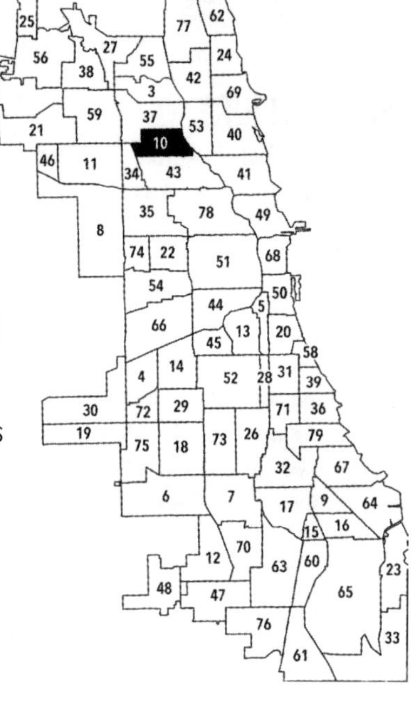


## DEMOGRAPHICS

Asian (3.2%), Black or African American (2.5%), Hispanic or Latino (65.8%), White (27.0%)

## LEARN

Avondale grew along Milwaukee Avenue and paralleling railroad lines, developing as a working-class community. Rapid growth began in 1889 following Avondale's annexation to Chicago. Transportation improved with the extension of street railway lines and the construction of the "L", providing means for commuting to the city for jobs. The rail lines and the river attracted industry in Avondale. The river banks once contained boatyards, brick factories, and an amusement park. Today, the industrial belt along the river is being replaced with luxury townhouses, condominiums, and shopping malls, leading to the loss of many industrial jobs that supported the working class for decades.[1]

## PRAY

Praise God for the diversity found in Avondale. Pray for ongoing unity between groups of people as the neighborhood continues to change.

The community as a whole is under-churched, and many of those who are involved in the church are more connected culturally than spiritually. Pray for an increased presence of the body of Christ in this neighborhood.

Unemployment and underemployment is a very real struggle in this community. Many households have parents working two or three jobs just to make ends meet. Pray for the physical, social, and emotional needs of these families.

The schools in this neighborhood attempt to educate the students, but face overcrowding and language barriers. Pray that despite these hurdles, resources would be allocated and the needs of the students would be met.

Pray for new businesses to focus on this area as there is still a need for economic improvement in the community.

1 Solzman, David M. Avondale. Encyclopedia of Chicago. http://encyclopedia.chicagohistory.org/pages/98.html.

# BELMONT CRAGIN

**ISAIAH 30:18**

*For the Lord is a God of justice . . .*

## NEIGHBORHOODS

Belmont Cragin, Brickyard, Cragin, Hanson Park

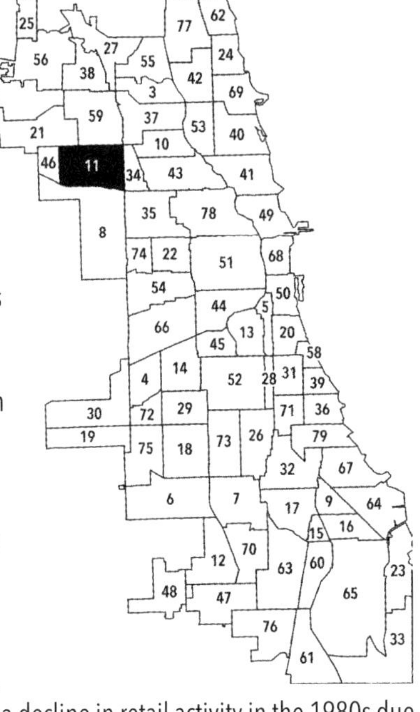


## DEMOGRAPHICS

Asian (1.8%), Black or African American (6.0%), Hispanic or Latino (72.4%), White (18.6%)

## LEARN

Belmont Cragin remained rural until 1882 when Cragin Brothers & Company, an iron processing plant, moved into the area. Job opportunities and rail service brought about a housing boom and an influx of settlers. Residents soon saw another boom when more factories in the 1920s were established in the area. The housing needs escalated, leading to the erection of bungalows, Cape Cods, and two-flats. The area continued to develop into the Post War years with the Chicago Transit Authority extension of its Belmont Street bus service and into the 1970s with continued construction of shopping malls and businesses. The Hispanic population also quadrupled from 1980 to 1990. Many Polish immigrants and businesses came to the area during these years. The area experienced a drop in manufacturing employment and a decline in retail activity in the 1980s due to shutting down of various plants. Residents organized home reinvestment and commercial development campaigns to confront the issues of unemployment and rising poverty.[1]

## PRAY

Thank God for a local nonprofit housing agency that was awarded a grant to address neighborhood housing concerns. Pray for the stabilization of the housing market as this neighborhood has been impacted by the large number of foreclosures.

Pray for increased civic involvement and the formation of block clubs, such as neighborhood watch, that help to establish a deeper level of safety in the community.

Pray for increased literacy in English and that this will help raise the standard of living for many.

Many instances of domestic abuse take place in this community, many that go unreported because of issues related to immigration. Pray for guidance for the churches and agencies addressing these numerous instances of domestic abuse in this area.

1 Perry, Marilyn Elizabeth. Belmont Cragin. Encyclodepia of Chicago. http://encyclopedia.chicagohistory.org/pages/129.html.

# √BEVERLY

**1 PETER 2:12**

*. . . they may on account of your good deeds . . . glorify God . . .*

## NEIGHBORHOODS

Beverly, West Beverly

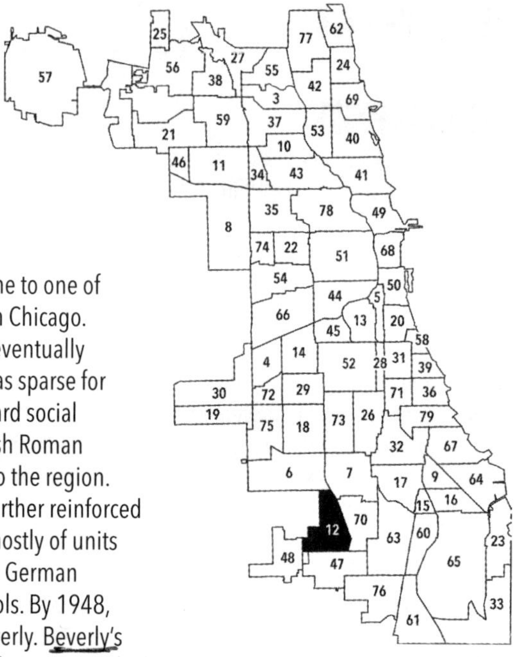

## DEMOGRAPHICS

Asian (0.5%), Black or African American (31.9%), Hispanic or Latino (3.1%), White (62.6%)

## LEARN

Beverly is a racially integrated neighborhood, home to one of the most stable middle-class residential districts in Chicago. Initially part of Washington Heights, Beverly was eventually annexed to Chicago in 1890, but its population was sparse for several decades. The community symbolized upward social mobility for European immigrants and later for Irish Roman Catholics and African Americans who migrated into the region. The community is primarily suburban in nature, further reinforced by Ridge Park. Consequently, housing consisted mostly of units for single families. In the 1920s, Irish Catholic and German Lutheran migrants established churches and schools. By 1948, Catholics became the largest denomination in Beverly. Beverly's population increased dramatically following World War II, mostly due to racial changes in neighborhoods like Englewood, Normal Park, and South Shore. In recent years, Beverly has experienced a slow decline in population and increased ethnic diversity.[1]

## PRAY

Beverly is one of the more diverse neighborhoods on the South Side. Pray for continued harmony among these different people groups.

Many neighborhood residents and retirees have been impacted by Chicago's budget challenges. Pray for the provision of their basic needs.

Pray for the stability of home values that have been hit hard by the recent housing downturn.

Many residents in this neighborhood are able to choose private schooling for their children. Pray that these schools would have a positive impact on the lives of the children.

1 Skerrett, Ellen. Beverly. Encyclopedia of Chicago. http://encyclopedia.chicagohistory.org/pages/134.html.

# ✓BRIDGEPORT

**JOHN 17:21**

*. . . that they may all be one . . . that the world may believe . . .*

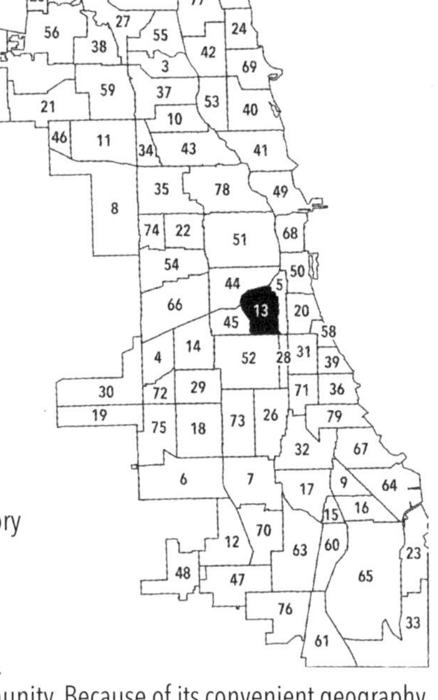


## NEIGHBORHOODS

Bridgeport

## DEMOGRAPHICS

Asian (32.4%), Black or African American (0.8%), Hispanic or Latino (27.0%), White (38.5%)

## LEARN

It was the Illinois & Michigan Canal in 1836 that awakened the first activity in the area of Chicago named Bridgeport. Lumber yards, manufacturing plants, and packinghouses opened along the river and canal as Bridgeport residents primarily worked in local industries. Residents began to see some change after the Civil War through municipal government employment. The neighborhood has also been home to five mayors, including Richard J. and Richard M. Daley. Also a part of Bridgeport's history is racial and ethnic conflict: clashes between Germans and the Irish in 1856, pro-Confederate rallies during the Civil War, and Polish and Lithuanian gangs in the twentieth century have all had their strife. The number of Mexican and Chinese residents has grown, as Bridgeport remains a largely working-class community. Because of its convenient geography in direct line to the Loop, Bridgeport maintains a high possibility for future investment and development. In addition, the rise of the artist community has started to have its stake in this growing neighborhood, changing the cultural climate of the area.[1]

## PRAY

As a growing ethnic community, Bridgeport is moving from a predominantly Irish and Italian community to a Chinese and Hispanic community. There is also a small pocket of Lithuanians living in the neighborhood. Pray for the emerging immigrant population and for their equal representation in the government.

Bridgeport continues to be the home of many of the city's workers and political leaders. Pray for wisdom and godly leadership in the government.

There are a number of Catholic churches as well as a Buddhist temple. Pray for the grace and truth of the gospel to penetrate the neighborhood and reach those who come from different religious backgrounds.

1 Pacyga, Dominic A. Bridgeport. Encyclopedia of Chicago. http://encyclopedia.chicagohistory.org/pages/165.html.

# BRIGHTON PARK

**JEREMIAH 22:16**

*He pled the cause of the afflicted . . .*
*"Is that not what it means to know Me?" declares the Lord.*

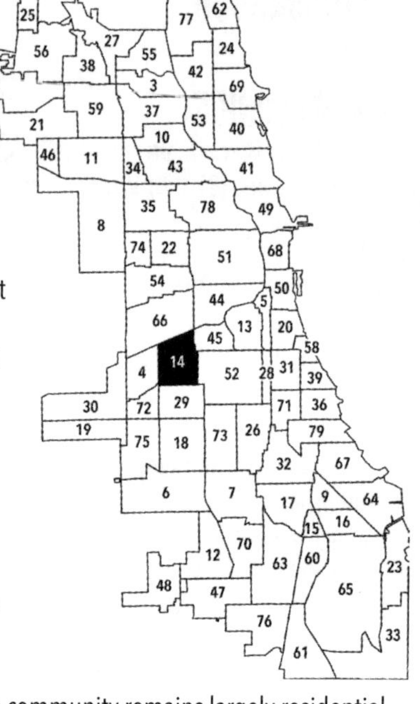


## NEIGHBORHOODS

Brighton Park

## DEMOGRAPHICS

Asian (5.5%), Black or African American (1.1%), Hispanic or Latino (82.0%), White (10.8%)

## LEARN

Brighton Park, taking its name from the Brighton livestock market in England, became a center for livestock trading in the late 1850s. Although the completion of the Union Stock Yard in 1865 closed Brighton's yards, the area attracted many other industries and mills. Brighton Park was annexed to the city of Chicago in 1889. By the 1880s and 1890s, infrastructure and transportation improvements drew a diverse population of French and Eastern European Jews, Poles, Lithuanians, and Italians. Industrial parks began opening in 1905, creating more jobs and leading to population growth in Brighton Park, which steadily became more residential. Between 1930 and 1980, however, Brighton Park's population significantly declined due to deindustrialization and the closing of Crane Manufacturing Company. To this day, the community remains largely residential and has a growing commercial section. By 2000, the population boomed again due to a large Hispanic movement into the neighborhood.[1]

## PRAY

Praise God for the existing churches in this community. Pray for their unity and a continued focus on evangelism.

Gang influence and teen pregnancy rates are very high at the local high school. Pray for transformation in the neighborhood, that it would be a place where young people can safely learn and grow.

Brighton Park was once full of blue collar work, but much of those jobs are no longer available. Pray for the provision of employment for the residents.

Pray for an increase of the spiritual temperature of the believers in the neighborhood. Pray that they would hunger and thirst to see God's kingdom come in Brighton Park as it is in heaven.

1 Stockwell, Clinton E. Brighton Park. Encyclopedia of Chicago. http://encyclopedia.chicagohistory.org/pages/168.html.

# BURNSIDE

**ACTS 10:38**

*You know of Jesus of Nazareth . . . He went about doing good . . .*

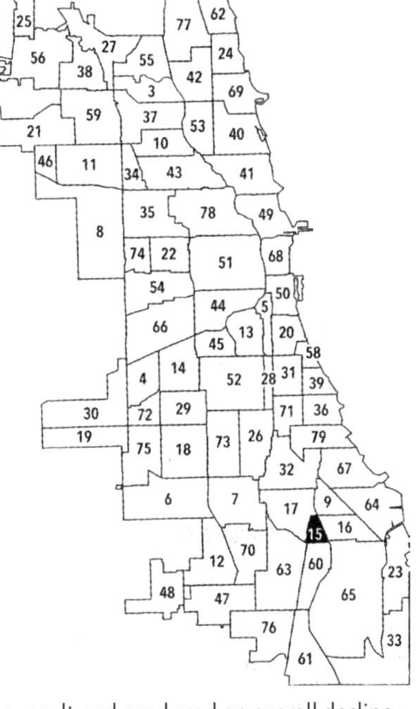


## NEIGHBORHOODS

Burnside

## DEMOGRAPHICS

Asian (0%), Black or African American (98.0%), Hispanic or Latino (0%), White (2.0%)

## LEARN

If you haven't heard of Burnside, it may come as no surprise, as this is the smallest of Chicago's community areas. It is bound entirely by railroads and like many neighborhoods in Chicago, it began development as a result of the Industrial Revolution. As the climate of this area changed to adapt to industrialization, more and more immigrants relocated to this area in hopes of finding work in the factories. Still, Burnside did not attract outside attention until after World War II and new single-family homes began to spring up. In the 1960s, African Americans started building or occupying homes in the area. Not uncommon to many South Side neighborhoods, Burnside began to fall under scrutiny of the Federal Housing Authority, with many loan scandals. A high number of foreclosures came as a result and produced an overall decline in the community. By the end of the twentieth century, Burnside became a more comfortable residential community, but once again, the area is experiencing more economic instability.[1]

## PRAY

Public transportation options have been limited in this community, despite being bordered by the tracks.

Pray against the marginalization of this community.

Schools have recently been labeled as underperforming in the neighborhood. Pray that the teachers and administrators could lead with vision and courage.

Burnside is showing signs of deterioration in recent years. Pray for economic revitalization in the area. Pray for Christ-followers in the community to take hope and reinvigorate the neighborhood.

1 Reiff, Janice L. Burnside. Encyclopedia of Chicago. http://encyclopedia.chicagohistory.org/pages/194.html.

# CALUMET HEIGHTS

**DEUTERONOMY 24:17**

*You shall not pervert the justice due an alien or an orphan . . .*

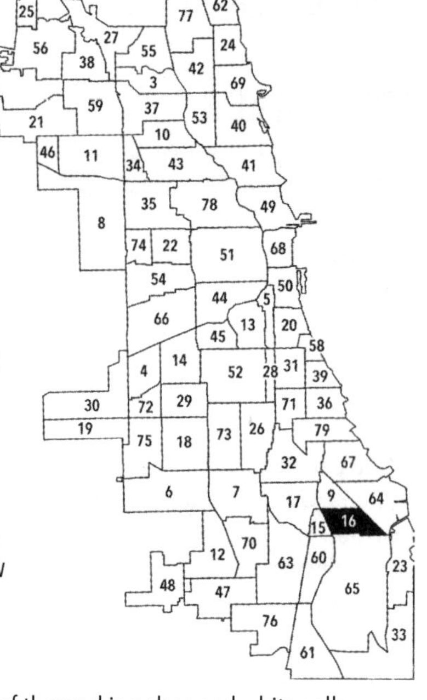


## NEIGHBORHOODS

Calumet Heights, Pill Hill

## DEMOGRAPHICS

Asian (0.5%), Black or African American (94.6%), Hispanic or Latino (4.3%), White (0.5%)

## LEARN

For the majority of the nineteenth century, Calumet Heights remained swampy and largely unoccupied. Not an unfamiliar story, the community dramatically changed with the construction of railroads. A quarry was built and the Calumet and Chicago Canal and Dock Company made its home nearby. Following these developments, real estate developers began to draw their attention to Calumet Heights, and by 1920, it became home to more than 3,000 residents, many of whom were Italian and Irish. In 1930, the population doubled with the establishment of a new commercial area. Between 1960 and 1980, the neighborhood experienced white flight, which resulted in a more than 86 percent African American population. Since that time, the area has remained a strong middle-class, as it became home to much of the working class and white collar employees who sought out the well-kept homes. The most affluent of these, making their home in "Pill Hill," which draws its name from the large community of doctors settling here due to its location near Advocate Trinity Hospital in South Chicago.[1]

## PRAY

Praise God for the large number of medical doctors who call this community their home and bring economic stability to the neighborhood. Pray for them as they care for patients throughout the Chicago area.

Pray for the capacity of local churches to bring together the resourced and underresourced within the community.

Pray against the enemy who is seeking to draw a larger presence of gangs, violence, and drugs to this neighborhood.

1 Patterson, Elizabeth A. Calumet Heights. Encyclopedia of Chicago. http://encyclopedia.chicagohistory.org/pages/200.html.

# √CHATHAM

**COLOSSIANS 1:9-10**

*. . . we have not ceased to pray for you and to ask that you . . . bear fruit in every good work*

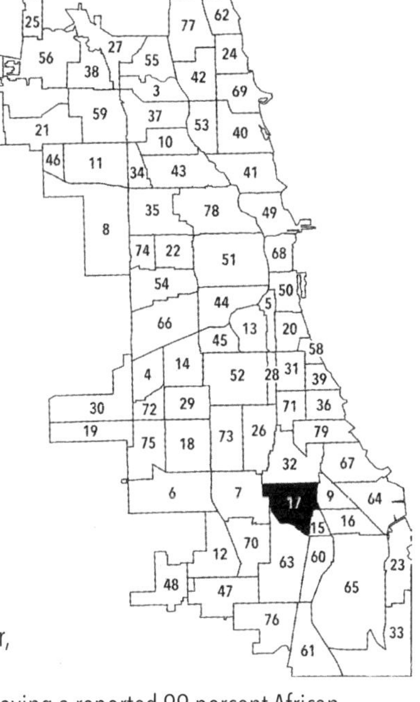


## NEIGHBORHOODS

Chatham, West Chesterfield

## DEMOGRAPHICS

Asian (0.3%), Black or African American (97.1%), Hispanic or Latino (0.3%), White (0.6%)

## LEARN

Business slowly reached Chatham in the early 1900s with steel mills, masonry, and the railroad that supplied jobs to European settlers in Chatham. By 1920, Chatham experienced an increase in population from 9,774 to 36,228. Then, after the Great Depression, the African American population increased from 1 percent in 1950 to 64 percent by 1960. Learning from the violence that took place in other communities, there was much less resistance to the change of demographic from the community. Churches welcomed the new residents into their churches and the Chatham-Avalon Park Community Council began to allow African Americans into the organization. However, due mostly to the scare tactics of some real estate agents, many of the previous European settlers moved out of the area leaving a reported 99 percent African American population in Chatham in 1990. The newly settled African American population worked hard to maintain the middle-class character of Chatham, and many successful businessmen have come from the neighborhood.[1]

## PRAY

New residents are moving into the area due to the closings of housing projects in other parts of the city. Pray that these new residents will take on the values of respect and care for others and the neighborhood and that crime will not gain a foothold in this community.

Pray for the elderly residents of Chatham, many of whom are widows and widowers. Pray that they may find community and would not feel overlooked in their later years. Also praise God for the people who are providing for their care.

As the community is beginning to experience socioeconomic transition, pray that class struggles would not cause division among the residents.

1 Best, Wallace. Chatham. Encyclopedia of Chicago. http://www.encyclopedia.chicagohistory.org/pages/232.html.

# CHICAGO LAWN

**EPHESIANS 4:3**

*. . . being diligent to preserve the unity of the Spirit in the bond of peace.*

## NEIGHBORHOODS

Chicago Lawn, Lithuanian Plaza, Marquette Park

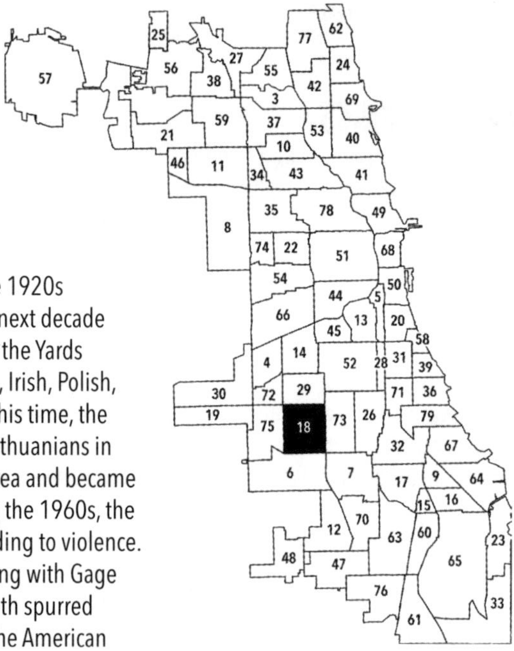

## DEMOGRAPHICS

Asian (0.5%), Black or African American (56.0%), Hispanic or Latino (37.2%), White (5.3%)

## LEARN

Chicago Lawn remained mostly farmland until the 1920s when stockyard workers moved into the area. The next decade marked an influx of ethnic groups leaving Back of the Yards and Englewood, including immigrants of German, Irish, Polish, Bohemian, and Lithuanian backgrounds. During this time, the population jumped from 14,000 to 47,000. The Lithuanians in particular established several institutions in the area and became a prominent identity within Chicago Lawn. During the 1960s, the area became a hotspot for racial tension often leading to violence. A march led in 1966 by Martin Luther King, Jr. along with Gage Park High School's attempt at racial integration both spurred racial violence. Aiming to escalate racial tension, the American Nazi Party also set up headquarters in Chicago Lawn, although short-lived. The racial population of Chicago Lawn continued to fluctuate. Various groups currently work diligently to keep this ethnically diverse neighborhood both economically healthy and racially peaceful.[1]

## PRAY

This community has a long history of racial division from the civil rights movement to the present day. Pray for the healing of long-standing wounds.

Gangs, drugs, and the underground economy of that lifestyle are a driving force in this community. Pray for a release from this bondage.

Foreclosures and boarded-up and abandoned housing contribute to a challenging real estate environment for home owners. Pray for relief economically.

Pray for city workers with conviction, vision, and influence to begin meeting the many needs of this community.

1 McMahon, Eileen M. Chicago Lawn. Encyclopedia of Chicago. http://encyclopedia.chicagohistory.org/pages/256.html.

# CLEARING

**MATTHEW 25:40**

*. . . to the extent that you did it to . . .*
*the least of them, you did it to Me.*

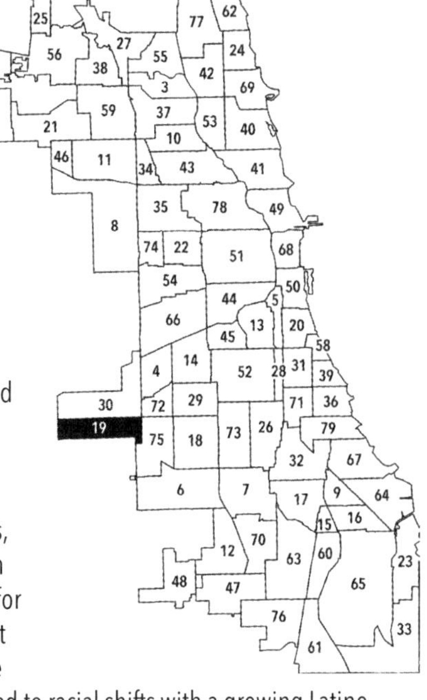


## NEIGHBORHOODS

Chrysler Village, Clearing

## DEMOGRAPHICS

Asian (0.7%), Black or African American (0.7%), Hispanic or Latino (40.5%), White (57.7%)

## LEARN

Clearing's name came from a proposed railway switching yard that would clear railway traffic in downtown Chicago. The plan failed, but the name remained. Eighteen industries in the area grew to more than ninety by 1928, and in 1926, land was leased to the city for the purpose of building the Chicago Municipal Airport. In 1949, the airport was renamed Midway Airport to honor victories at Midway Island during World War II. Clearing entered a postwar residential and economic boom in the 1940s, which reached its peak by 1970. During the economic recession from 1974 to 1984, over half of the companies in Clearing left for other locations. With the resurgence of Midway Airport in recent years, much of the stability that was lost has been regained. The most recent transition Clearing has experienced has been related to racial shifts with a growing Latino population.[1]

## PRAY

Praise God for the economic stability provided by the Midway Airport. Pray for more employment opportunities for residents.

While most residents have jobs, many are underpaid. Pray for the many underemployed residents and their families.

This community has a large population of Latino and Polish immigrants. Pray for the immigration reform deliberations that will directly impact these residents.

Pray for the unity of the Clearing residents who are impacted by the separation of many family members due to immigration proceedings.

1 Stockwell, Clinton E. Clearing. Encyclopedia of Chicago. http://encyclopedia.chicagohistory.org/pages/296.html.

# DOUGLAS

**MATTHEW 5:16**

*Let your light shine . . . that they may see your good works . . .*

## NEIGHBORHOODS

Bronzeville, Douglas, The Gap

## DEMOGRAPHICS

Asian (7.1%), Black or African American (77.4%), Hispanic or Latino (1.9%), White (13.2%)

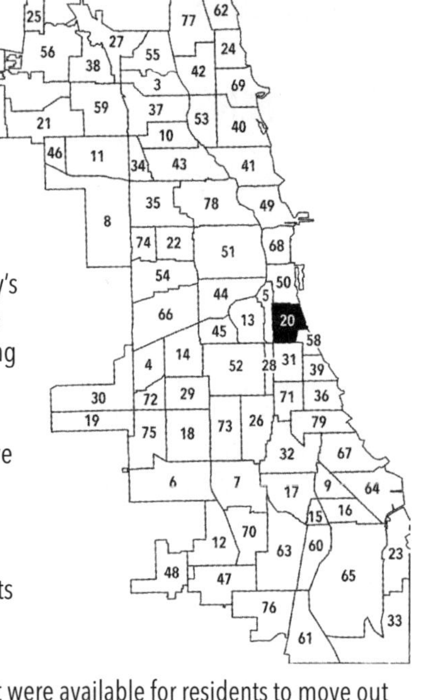


## LEARN

In the early 1880s and 1890s, Douglas attracted many of the city's leading Jewish families and many working-class families. By the 1890s, African Americans also starting moving into the area along the narrow strip called the "Black Belt." In the 1920s, Douglas became the hub of African American business and cultural life. This area, known as Bronzevillle or the Black Metropolis, was alive with a diversification of professional and commercial interests, but took a major hit after the stock market crash of 1929. Most businesses closed due to the segregated housing market. The Chicago Housing Authority (CHA) developed the housing projects which were still not sufficient to house the 30,000 new African Americans that moved to the area during World War II. Violence and intimidation by white Chicagoans restricted the options that were available for residents to move out of the community. As a result, even more housing was constructed by the CHA in the 1950s and 1960s. Since the 1980s, there has been considerable effort to restore the once vibrant culture and business with considerable success, as Douglas now boasts a strong middle class, green scenery, and easy access to downtown venues.[1]

## PRAY

Praise the Lord for the numerous African American churches in the neighborhood that have persevered in their presence and witness within the community.

The past decade has seen a dramatic decrease in population. This has resulted in the closings and mergers of multiple schools. Pray for stability in the community and renewed educational growth.

The lack of economic development has led to stagnant property values. Pray for development that would increase people's investments and bring new opportunities for members of the community.

There is a wide range of income levels in the community. Pray for unity among people of different socio-economic levels.

1 Capeheart, Adrian. Douglas. Encyclopedia of Chicago. http://encyclopedia.chicagohistory.org/pages/388.html.

# DUNNING

**PSALM 127:1**

*. . . unless the Lord guards the city, the watchman keeps awake in vain.*

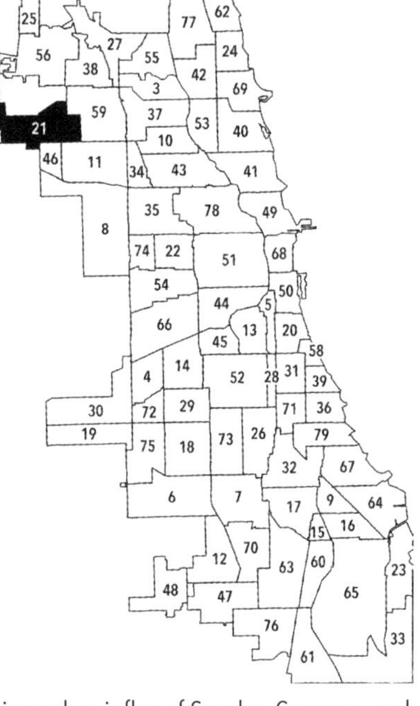


## NEIGHBORHOODS

Belmont Heights, Belmont Terrace, Dunning, Irving Woods, Schorsch Village

## DEMOGRAPHICS

Asian (3.8%), Black or African American (1.2%), Hispanic or Latino (20.6%), White (73.2%)

## LEARN

In 1851, Dunning was reserved by the County for a poor farm and a mental health facility, due to its remote location. More buildings were erected in the 1880s to accommodate the more than one thousand patients. Following the Civil War, Andrew Dunning attempted to form a settlement, but proximity to the facility kept people away. Shoddy living conditions, such as poor heating and insufficient ventilation, contributed to the deaths of many patients. Official investigations also revealed misconduct, gambling, and patient abuse within the facility. Thus, in 1910, the poor house was moved to Oak Forest while the hospital was bought by the state for one dollar. Outside the facility, the population grew only to 1,305. After World War I, Dunning experienced an influx of Swedes, Germans, and Poles. Colleges and other institutions were established, and the population peaked to 43,856 in 1970. In the decade following, the State Hospital was re-constructed as the Chicago-Read Mental Health Center. During the 1980s and 1990s, Dunning experienced significant institutional, commercial, and residential growth and became a popular location for residents, with luxury homes and modern facilities. By 2000, the population reached 42,164.[1]

## PRAY

Pray for the residents to have a growing curiosity, fresh eyes, and open hearts to the local churches.

Pray for families in the community, especially for parents to be involved in the lives of their children and to model wholesome values.

Pray for the body of Christ to give time, resources, and people to engage the youth and teens in the community.

Pray for the healthcare providers in the neighborhood responding to mental and physical needs of their patients. Pray that they would be effective and compassionate in their care and treatment.

1 Perry, Mary Elizabeth. Dunning. Encyclopedia of Chicago. http://encyclopedia.chicagohistory.org/pages/395.html.

# √ EAST GARFIELD PARK

**DEUTERONOMY 15:11**

*. . . the poor will never cease to be in the land . . .*

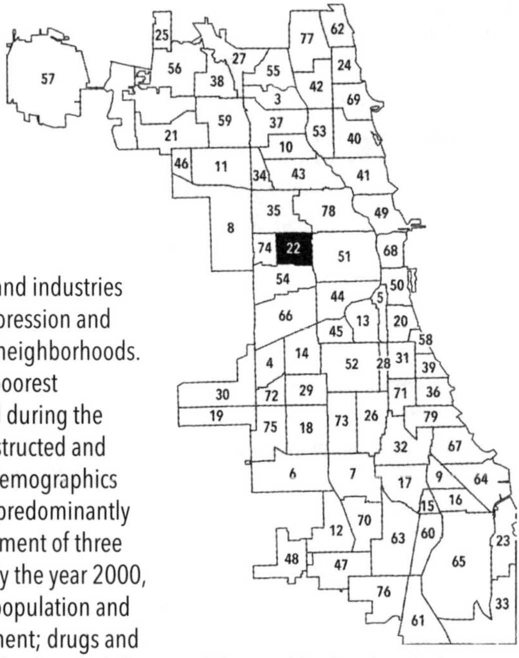

## NEIGHBORHOODS

East Garfield Park, Fifth City

## DEMOGRAPHICS

Asian (0.5%), Black or African American (93.1%), Hispanic or Latino (2.0%), White (3.4%)

## LEARN

Although modest homes, commercial buildings, and industries made up East Garfield Park in 1914, the Great Depression and WWII resulted in the deterioration of homes and neighborhoods. As a result, East Garfield Park became one of the poorest neighborhoods in the city. The situation worsened during the 1950s when the Eisenhower Expressway was constructed and displaced residents from a southern stretch. The demographics shifted from Irish, German, Italian, and Jewish to predominantly African American. The 1960s brought the development of three different housing projects in the neighborhood. By the year 2000, East Garfield had lost more than two-thirds of its population and was plagued by endemic poverty and unemployment; drugs and prostitution filled the economic void. High hopes for the rehabilitation of the neighborhood, including plans for a Madison Street revitalization initiative, have resulted in little improvement. The economy of East Garfield has never fully recovered, and the neighborhood continues to face many challenges with gang violence, drugs, and unemployment.[1]

## PRAY

There have been multiple shootings in East Garfield Park, especially near the corner of Lake and Homan. Pray for protection for children in the community and for the violence in the area to stop.

Ministries in the community are responding with holistic outreach programs, addressing the needs of youth, families, and the homeless. Pray that these ministries would continue being effective in the community.

The neighborhood is home to a refocused selective enrollment high school. With the recent school closings, pray that the children of East Garfield Park would be able to test into this school.

Pray for the staff members of local churches and ministries who experience vicarious trauma and fatigue as they listen to and wrestle with so many stories of hardship.

1 Seligman, Amanda. East Garfield Park. Encyclopedia of Chicago. http://www.encyclopedia.chicagohistory.org/pages/404.html.

# EAST SIDE

**PHILIPPIANS 2:3**

*. . . with humility of mind let each of you regard one another as more important than himself.*

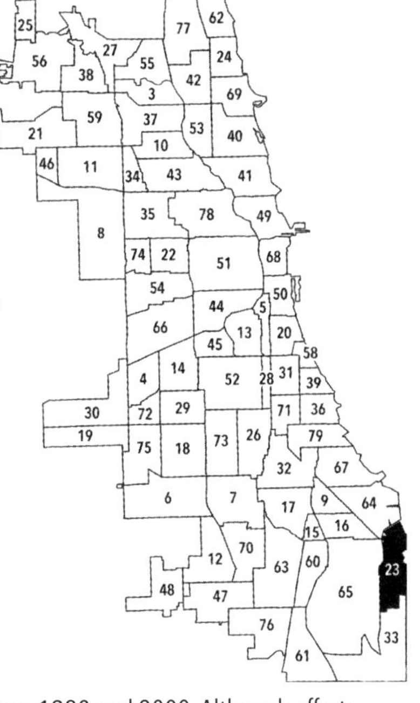


## NEIGHBORHOODS

East Side

## DEMOGRAPHICS

Asian (0.3%), Black or African American (2.3%), Hispanic or Latino (77.6%), White (19.4%)

## LEARN

Construction of the railroads originally drew many new residents to the area in the late 1800s. With the success of its industry, primarily steel production, the economy was strong and the population exploded. During that time, East Siders enjoyed a certain amount of voluntary social isolation being surrounded by water on three sides. Its family and friendship ties remained strong during this time, but racial tension following World War II brought great conflict to the area, including race riots, as African Americans started to settle in the area. The decline of the steel industry in Chicago also hit East Siders hard, bringing a decline to the economy and driving residents out of the neighborhood in search for employment. Much of the population that left was replaced with a Hispanic population that grew significantly between 1980 and 2000. Although efforts of revitalization have been made with the declaration of the East Side as an "enterprise zone" and the expansion of Ford Motor Company into the former Republic Steel site, the area continues to struggle economically.[1]

## PRAY

Many businesses have closed, resulting in empty buildings and the need to shop outside the neighborhood. Pray for the good use of existing structures and a renewed economy.

A new school is planned to ease overcrowding. Pray for timely completion of the project, community and parental involvement, and good role models in the schools.

Some older, established churches are struggling with upkeep of their facilities in light of aging and decreased constituencies. Pray for direction for congregations and denominations that will need to make hard decisions.

Pray for a renewed focus among the churches to build bridges into the large and growing Latino community in this neighborhood.

1 Bas, Kristian M. and David Bensman. East Side. Encyclopedia of Chicago. http://www.encyclopedia.chicagohistory.org/pages/406.html

# EDGEWATER

**TITUS 3:8**

*. . . so that those who have believed God may be careful to engage in good deeds . . .*

## NEIGHBORHOODS

Andersonville, Edgewater Glen, Epic, Lakewood/Balmoral

## DEMOGRAPHICS

Asian (10.4%), Black or African American (15.4%), Hispanic or Latino (13.7%), White (57.0%)

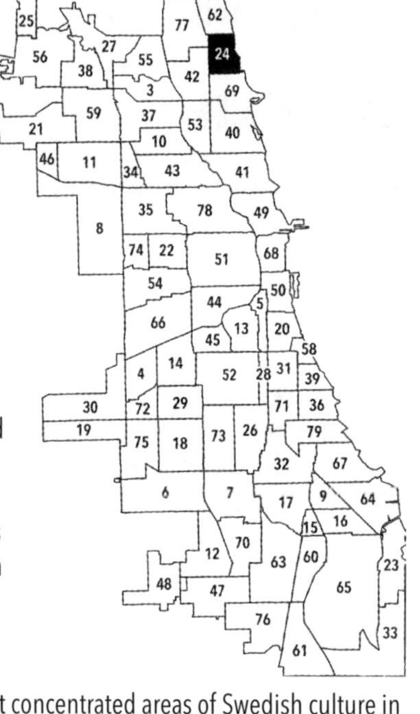


## LEARN

Currently the most densely populated neighborhood in Chicago, Edgewater's rapid growth began in 1886 due the railroad. However, with the citywide housing crisis in the 1940s, apartment buildings were later subdivided into smaller units and mansions were destroyed and replaced with high-rises. These developments led to the formation of the Edgewater Community Council (ECC) in 1960, established to initiate local improvements to combat the prospect of social and physical deterioration within Edgewater. During the 1970s, the ECC fought and succeeded to separate Edgewater from Uptown, which many property-owners regarded as the reason for Edgewater's backsliding.[1] Andersonville, a neighborhood of Edgewater, has one of the most concentrated areas of Swedish culture in the United States. It is also home to a diverse assortment of devoted residents and businesses, including one of Chicago's largest lesbian gay bisexual transgender (LGBT) communities and a thriving Hispanic commercial area.[2]

## PRAY

Many residents live in two or three flats only accessible to those in the building, making it a challenge to churches and ministries seeking to reach the community. Pray for creative access to these residents.

Andersonville is home to an extensive LGBT community. Pray for receptivity to caring and compassionate witnesses by Christ-followers over the long haul.

Edgewater is still a relatively unchurched community compared to the population density. Pray for newer church plants starting and an even greater dispersion of the gospel.

Praise God for growing unity among existing churches meeting regularly for prayer and planning to better serve the community.

1 Seligman, Amanda. Edgewater. Encyclopedia of Chicago. http://encyclopedia.chicagohistory.org/pages/413.html.

2 History of Andersonville. Andersonville Chamber of Commerce. http://www.andersonville.org/andersonville-chicago/history.

# EDISON PARK

**PSALM 46:4,5**

*. . . the city of God . . . God is in the midst of her . . .*
*God will help her . . .*

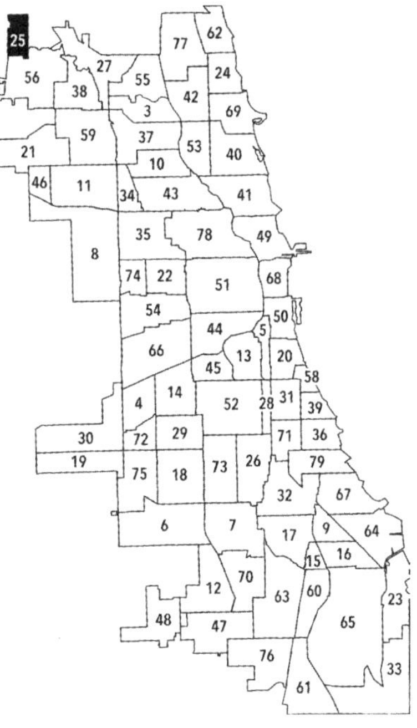


## NEIGHBORHOODS

Edison Park

## DEMOGRAPHICS

Asian (1.7%), Black or African American (0%), Hispanic or Latino (3.7%), White (93.6%)

## LEARN

Edison Park was predominantly filled with Native American tribes in the 1830s before German farmers claimed the land. The arrival of the railroad in the 1850s brought an influx of developers into the area. By 1910, the population rose to about 300 residents. Edison Park was eventually annexed to Chicago in 1910. A major building boom in Edison Park after World War I brought many second-generation immigrants, mostly Roman Catholic or Lutheran, into the area, and the population grew by over 400 percent as a result. The initial agricultural neighborhood soon became highly residential and industrial. Currently, the neighborhood boasts an easy commute to work, leisure, and shopping opportunities within the city and in the surrounding suburban areas.[1]

## PRAY

Edison Park is an extremely family-oriented neighborhood.

Pray that the children living in Edison Park will find Christ at an early age and for protection over marriages.

Many of the residents in Edison Park are homeowners and permanent residents. Pray for hospitable, servant attitudes among the believers in Edison Park.

Pray that they will see their home as a gift from the Lord and seek to use it to bless others in the community.

Pray that this area would see a true revival of Christianity rather than beliefs based on tradition. Pray for hearts to be compelled with the truth of the gospel.

1 Keating, Ann Durkin. Edison Park. Encyclopedia of Chicago. http://encyclopedia.chicagohistory.org/pages/414.html.

# ENGLEWOOD

**NEHEMIAH 1:3**

*. . . the wall of Jerusalem is broken down . . .*
*the remnant there are in great distress . . .*

## NEIGHBORHOODS

Englewood, Hamilton Park

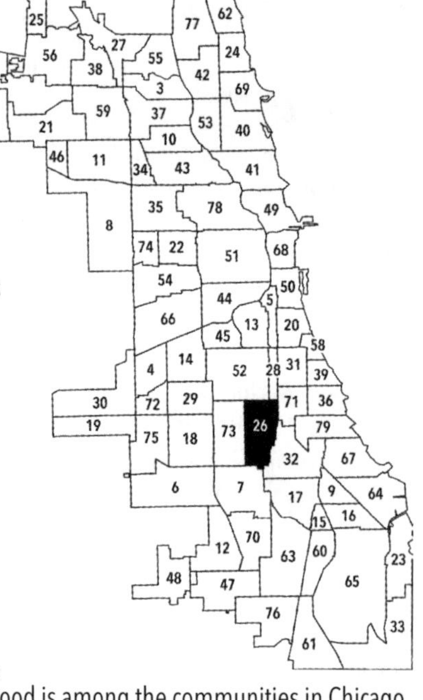


## DEMOGRAPHICS

Asian (0%), Black or African American (98.5%), Hispanic or Latino (0.4%), White (0.6%)

## LEARN

In 1920, Englewood's shopping district at Halsted and 63rd was the second busiest in the city. The 1940s began the decline of real estate values. The growing number of people moving from the east to Chicago's South Side resulted in a rapid turnover of the population in Englewood. Discriminatory practices such as redlining and disinvestment led to Englewood's transformation into a low-income community with housing on the decline. Additionally, redevelopment of Englewood was difficult due to the scarcity of the necessary materials following World War II. Between 1940 and 1970, the African American percentage of the population steadily increased to 96 percent. Attempts at restoring the shopping district remained unsuccessful. By 2010, Englewood's population declined to 30,654. To this day, Englewood is among the communities in Chicago that have suffered the greatest loss in housing stock and population and suffers from some of the highest rates of violence in Chicago.[1]

## PRAY

Pray that the youth organizations and churches that are serving the children of this community would be able to instill a desire to stay away from gangs, guns, and drugs, and to reestablish priorities that include deeper self-worth and identity in Christ.

City planners are focused on development in this area where local parents and young people could find gainful employment. Pray that this development would allow residents to make an honest living and would bring a positive economy to the area.

Praise God for the recently renovated Kennedy-King College in the heart of Englewood. Pray that God would use the presence of this school to cast a vision for higher education in the community.

Pray for the mobilization of God's people who are willing to walk the streets, build relationships, and invest human capital in the lives of this neighborhood.

1 Stockwell, Clinton E. Englewood. Encyclopedia of Chicago. http://encyclopedia.chicagohistory.org/pages/426.html.

# FOREST GLEN

**2 CHRONICLES 20:12**

*. . . For we are powerless before this great multitude . . .*
*but our eyes are on Thee.*

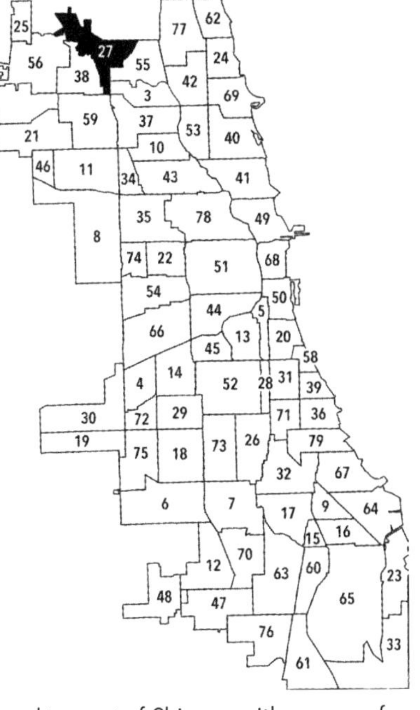


## NEIGHBORHOODS

Edgebrook, Forest Glen, Middle Edgebrook, Sauganash, Wildwood

## DEMOGRAPHICS

Asian (10.1%), Black or African American (1.6%)
Hispanic or Latino (12.6%), White (74.9%)

## LEARN

Forest Glen is home to many city administrators, lawyers, judges, and political figures. Forest Glen's far northwest locale secluded it from the city surrounded by forest preserves, parks, and the North Branch of the Chicago River. As Chicago urbanization grew outward, railroad stops at Forest Glen and Edgebrook ushered in commuter settlement by the 1880s. Progress was stilted by the relative seclusion of Forest Glen from the city until the 1920s, when home building was prioritized. By 1940, Forest Glen showed signs of being a wealthy community with fine homes, mostly residential in nature. There were few apartments or townhouses, though homes in the area were starkly diverse and stratified. Currently, the community continues to be stable, compared to most of Chicago, with a sense of political power. To this day, the area remains home to a majority white, Roman Catholic community.[1]

## PRAY

Pray for safety over the many men and women who live in this neighborhood and work in other parts of the city as firefighters and police officers.

Many people in Forest Glen are largely concerned with pursuing worldly success and fortune. Pray that God will create a spiritual thirst for the gospel resulting in people longing to follow Jesus Christ as their Lord and Savior.

Many residents in the community are busy with family and careers. Pray that they would be connected with a church body and dedicate their specific passions and giftings to be a positive influence in their community, workplaces, and families.

Pray for the elderly people who live here, that they would be treated with dignity and kindness by their neighbors and society at large.

1 Solzman, David M. Forest Glen. Encyclopedia of Chicago. http://encyclopedia.chicagohistory.org/pages/473.html.

# FULLER PARK

**MATT. 9:35**

*Jesus was going about all the cities . . . proclaiming the gospel . . .*

## NEIGHBORHOODS

Fuller Park

## DEMOGRAPHICS

Asian (0.3%), Black or African American (97.4%), Hispanic or Latino (0%), White (0.6%)

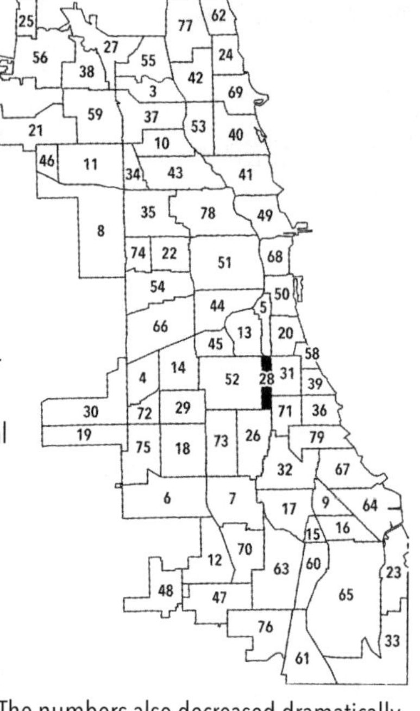


## LEARN

Fuller Park is one of Chicago's smallest community areas, encompassing a narrow two-mile strip. The community of Fuller Park was fairly poor from the beginning. After the Civil War, Fuller Park consisted of mostly Irish descendants, employed either by the railroads or stockyards. After the Great Fire in 1871, residential growth increased as developers hoped to avoid the expensive building codes found within the city. By 1920, African Americans, Mexicans, and Slavs had replaced the Irish and Germans. In the 1950s, the Dan Ryan Expressway overran and split the community, displacing a third of the population. Fuller Park underwent a huge population change from 80 percent white in 1945 to 97 percent black in 1970. The local economy was also hit hard during this time when the Union Stock Yard closed in 1971. The numbers also decreased dramatically from 17,000 to 4,000 by 1990. In the 1980s, Fuller Park received fewer bank loans for home improvement than any other neighborhood in Chicago. The poverty rate is over 40 percent, with single mothers leading a large number of these families. To this day, rehabilitation efforts are being made by neighbors of Fuller Park.[1]

## PRAY

Unemployment in this neighborhood impacts well over one-third of the residents. Pray for much needed economic development in order to provide jobs to its residents.

Over half of all households in Fuller Park live below the poverty level, which deeply affects the psyche of the residents. Pray for encouragement and a spirit of hope in the midst of such great need.

Community residents live in the shadow of high crime rates. Pray for safety and protection and a different path for people to take other than violence.

1 Stockwell, Clinton E. Fuller Park. Encyclopedia of Chicago. http://encyclopedia.chicagohistory.org/pages/490.html.

# GAGE PARK

**ACTS 1:14**

*These all with one mind were continually devoting themselves to prayer . . .*

## NEIGHBORHOODS

Gage Park

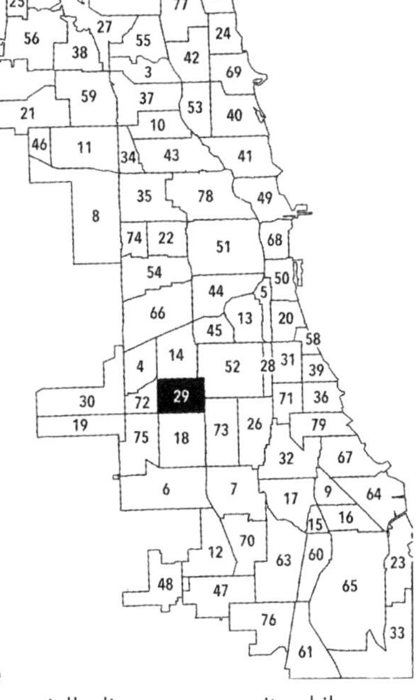


## DEMOGRAPHICS

Asian (0.4%), Black or African American (5.7%), Hispanic or Latino (85.7%), White (7.2%)

## LEARN

At the time Gage Park was annexed to Chicago in 1889, the town consisted of thirty wood-framed cottages with no paved streets. Once the electric trolley was extended to Gage Park in the early 1900s, the area experienced a building boom with increased industrial and residential development. The area was made up of mainly Bohemian and Polish residents, many who were faithful to the Roman Catholic Church. Decades later, Gage Park was influenced greatly by racial and civil unrest. It became the focal point for piloting open housing for African Americans and was the site of a march led by Dr. Martin Luther King, Jr. that was met with violent resistance. In the 1970s and 1980s, several neighborhood organizations formed in order to neutralize and ease racial tension. As a result of these efforts, Gage Park was a racially diverse community while maintaining an established middle-class. More recently, the Latino population has rapidly increased and is now the dominant ethnic group.[1]

## PRAY

Many deaths have come as a result of gang affiliation in Gage Park. Pray against the history of violence that exists in the neighborhood.

Many people in Gage Park do not speak English, making it difficult to secure employment and adapt to the culture in the United States. Pray that the Latino population in this areas would know how to make Gage Park their home and find employment.

Pray for the provision of education, financial, and social assistance so that opportunities will be available to the community residents.

Pray for those who are combating the system to become legal citizens through the immigration challenges.

1 Stockwell, Clinton E. Gage Park. Encyclopedia of Chicago. http://encyclopedia.chicagohistory.org/pages/494.html.

# GARFIELD RIDGE

**MARK 1:35**

*. . . He arose and went out . . . to a lonely place, and was praying there.*

## NEIGHBORHOODS

Le Claire Courts, Sleepy Hollow, Vittum Park

## DEMOGRAPHICS

Asian (2.3%), Black or African American (7.5%), Hispanic or Latino (33.5%), White (56.1%)

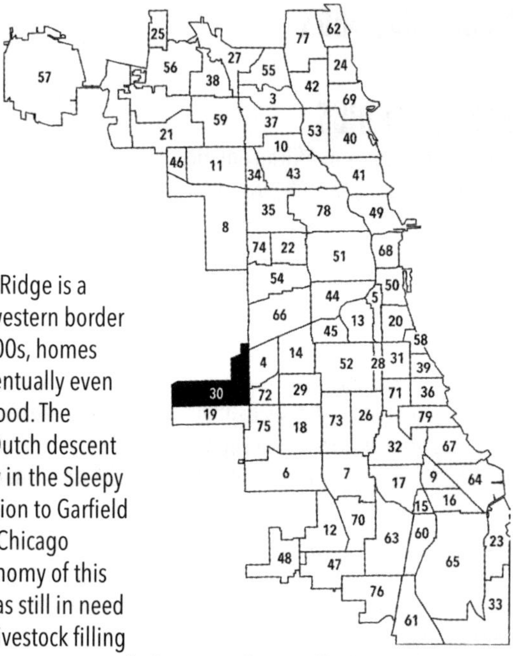

## LEARN

Previously under the name Archer Limits, Garfield Ridge is a well-established family neighborhood along the western border of the city. With the rise of industrialism in the 1900s, homes sprouted up, making this area very residential, eventually even surpassing the industrial aspect of this neighborhood. The majority of Garfield Ridge's early settlers were of Dutch descent and made their living as market gardeners, mostly in the Sleepy Hollow neighborhood. Probably the greatest addition to Garfield Ridge happened in 1926 with the opening of the Chicago Municipal Airport, now known as Midway. The economy of this community was set, although by appearances it was still in need of development with dirt roads, farmhouses, and livestock filling the area. With the establishment of O'Hare Airport came a great decline in Midway traffic, but in the 1990s, people began to turn their eyes again to Midway and with the arrival of easy transit to the Loop. Garfield Ridge has held strong and continued to grow as an urban community.[1]

## PRAY

Praise God for Midway Airport, the economic hub of the community. Pray for its continued vitality.

Thank God for a history of stability of family-centered homes and schools. Pray that this culture would survive and thrive.

The teenage dropout rate in this community is on the rise. Pray for families to encourage their students and that these teenagers would understand the importance of a good education.

In the last decade, many Latino residents have been moving into the community. Pray for acceptance and unity within this diverse atmosphere.

1 Keyes, Johnathan. Garfield Ridge. Encyclopedia of Chicago. http://encyclopedia.chicagohistory.org/pages/501.html.

# GRAND BOULEVARD

**PROVERBS 14:21**

*. . . happy is he who is gracious to the poor.*

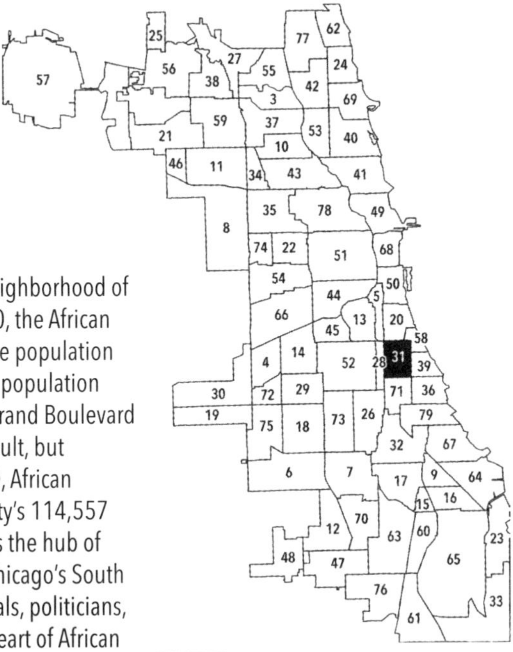

## NEIGHBORHOODS

Grand Boulevard

## DEMOGRAPHICS

Asian (0.2%), Black or African American (93.7%), Hispanic or Latino (1.1%), White (3.6%)

## LEARN

By the early 1900s, Grand Boulevard became a neighborhood of many middle- and working-class families. By 1920, the African American community constituted 32 percent of the population and increased dramatically with 95 percent of the population being African American by 1930. Unfortunately, Grand Boulevard experienced racial resistance and violence as a result, but nevertheless, the community thrived and by 1950, African Americans comprised 99 percent of the community's 114,557 residents. Grand Boulevard also became known as the hub of Bronzeville, an African American community on Chicago's South Side. The community thrived with black intellectuals, politicians, sports figures, artists, writers, and it became the heart of African American culture in Chicago. Unfortunately, the prosperity Grand Boulevard formally enjoyed does not describe this area any longer. This neighborhood is now categorized as one of high unemployment rates, poverty, and physical decline. In the 1990s, two-thirds of the community population was living in poverty, and Grand Boulevard held the highest population of public housing in America. Currently there are many organizations striving to meet the needs of Grand Boulevard and its inhabitants.[1]

## PRAY

Many developers are working to bring new housing to the neighborhood. Pray that these organizations would create affordable units that would lead to a self-sustaining community.

Also pray that at this point when Grand Boulevard could experience change or development that it would be done with consideration to those who have resided there for many years.

Pray that the Lord will raise up men and women to create businesses in this area to give back to the community.

Pray for a display of the true gospel from the churches within the community. Pray that the people will experience a deep relationship with Christ and not just follow tradition.

1 Best, Wallace. Grand Boulevard. Encyclopedia of Chicago. http://encyclopedia.chicagohistory.org/pages/537.html.

# √GREATER GRAND CROSSING

**PROVERBS 31:9**

*. . . defend the rights of the afflicted and needy.*

## NEIGHBORHOODS

Brookdale, Brookline, Essex, Grand Crossing, Greater Grand Crossing, Park Manor

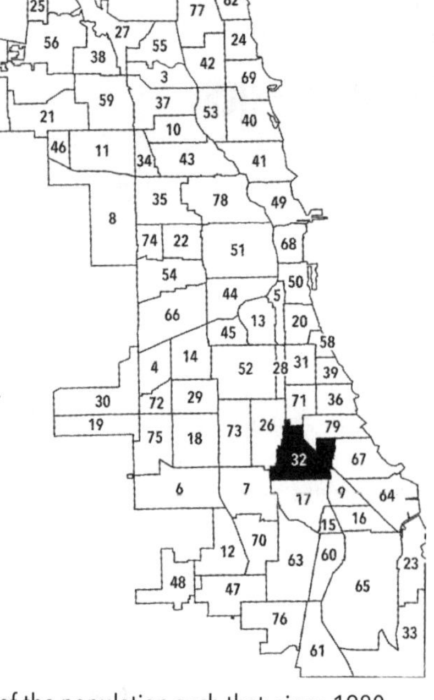


## DEMOGRAPHICS

Asian (0.1%), Black or African American (97.4%), Hispanic or Latino (0.6%), White (1.3%)

## LEARN

Greater Grand Crossing was annexed to Chicago in 1889, and encompasses several neighborhoods. Development in this area began after a train accident in 1853 that killed eighteen people. Early settlers were of Irish, English, and Scottish backgrounds. Many German immigrants came into the area during the 1890s. The World's Columbian Exposition of 1893 further stimulated population growth, and many single-family homes and apartments appeared during this time. The infrastructure of railways was improved as well. During the 1930s, African Americans came into the community, while white and other ethnic groups began to move out. During the 1950s, the black population increased dramatically from 6 percent to 86 percent of the population such that, since 1980, the community's demographic has been almost 99 percent African American. There has been little construction in Greater Grand Crossing since the 1960s, and as of 1990, a fifth of the population lived at or below poverty level. However, about a third of the residents were second- and third-generation property owners.[1]

## PRAY

Pray for the Spirit to move through this community that has been sadly neglected spiritually and economically for decades.

Pray for the churches and ministries to grab hold of this neighborhood and keep it out of the clutches of violence.

Pray for financial stability for struggling families in the community.

Praise God that despite the hardships the community has faced, over a third of residents are second- or third-generation property owners.

1 Best, Wallace. Greater Grand Crossing. Encyclopedia of Chicago. http://www.encyclopedia.chicagohistory.org/pages/547.html.

# HEGEWISCH

**GALATIANS 6:10**

*. . . while we have opportunity, let us do good to all men . . .*

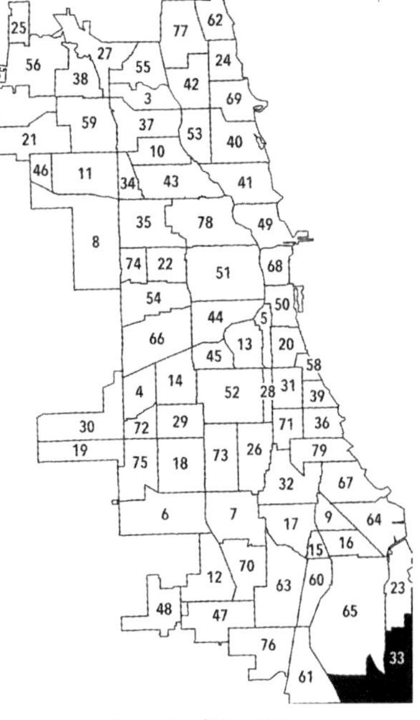

## NEIGHBORHOODS

Hegewisch

## DEMOGRAPHICS

Asian (0.1%), Black or African American (7.1%), Hispanic or Latino (43.3%), White (48.9%)

## LEARN

Steel mills formed the backbone of Hegewisch's economic development since its annexation to Chicago in 1889. During the heart of the Industrial Revolution, there were many attempts to organize employees to improve the poor conditions in the steel mills, resulting in a number of strikes, some resulting in violence. The most famous of these outbreaks is now known as the Memorial Day Massacre when off-duty police officers hired by Republic Steel opened fire on the nonviolent demonstrators, killing ten and injuring hundreds more. After World War II, steel manufacturing took a major decline across the U.S., causing many to move out of Hegewisch. However, the residents came up with creative ways to counteract the loss of one industry by focusing their efforts on renewal projects. They lobbied for a Metra stop, a branch of the Chicago Public Library, and a large block grant for infrastructure repairs. Currently, the residents of Hegewisch are employed by various industries, including DMC, a major Midwest distributor of Ford automobiles, and nearby Indiana casinos.[1]

## PRAY

There is a strong presence of gang members in Hegewisch. Pray that no more gang members would move into this area and gang members who already live there would find freedom from that lifestyle.

Struggles with depression and hopelessness have resulted in a great deal of drug and alcohol abuse. Pray for the body of Christ to minister hope and reach out in caring ways.

The younger and middle-aged residents have become disillusioned with religion and are ripe for the gospel. Pray that they would discover a true relationship with Jesus Christ.

The neighborhood is in close proximity to a number of casinos. Pray that residents would not fall prey to the bondage of gambling.

1 Gellman, Erik. Hegewisch. Encyclopedia of Chicago. http://encyclopedia.chicagohistory.org/pages/577.html.

# HERMOSA

**PSALM 5:3**

*. . . I will order my prayer to Thee and eagerly watch.*

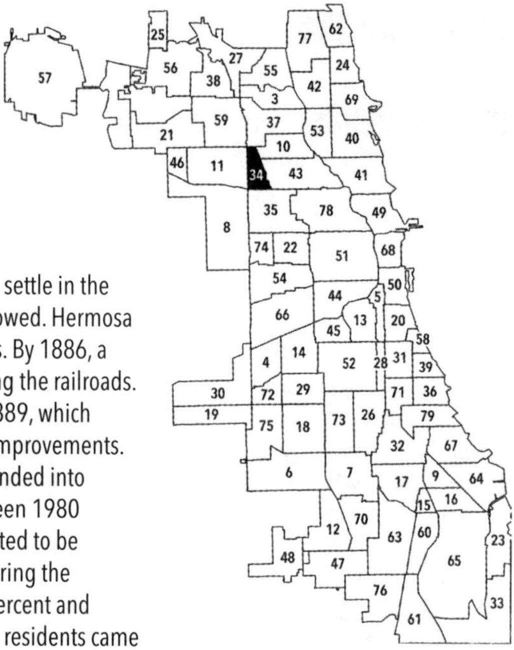

## NEIGHBORHOODS

Belmont Gardens, Hermosa, Kelvyn Park

## DEMOGRAPHICS

Asian (2.6%), Black or African American (1.7%), Hispanic or Latino (84.9%), White (10.1%)

## LEARN

In the 1880s, Scottish immigrants were the first to settle in the area. German and Scandinavian farmers soon followed. Hermosa continued to grow due to industrial developments. By 1886, a good number of companies were established along the railroads. Hermosa was eventually annexed to Chicago in 1889, which brought about slow municipal service and street improvements. Growth accelerated when streetcar lines were extended into the community. Hermosa's population grew between 1980 and 1990, during which ethnic demographics shifted to be more Hispanic in nature. Crime rates increased during the 1970s. Around 1990, poverty rates were at 17.4 percent and unemployment rates at 10.9 percent. In response, residents came together as block clubs, church groups, and organizations to voice concerns and take action against further deterioration in the neighborhood. These groups worked to combat gang problems and raise concerns about subsidized housing.[1]

## PRAY

The high school dropout rate in Hermosa is very high. Pray for the youth in the schools to desire a bright future that could be accomplished by staying in school and for the support and encouragement from family and friends.

Many residents in Hermosa come from families with mothers as the head of the household, many of whom are very young. Pray that these young women would find their identity in the Lord instead of finding security and identity in men.

Drugs, alcohol, and gangs are getting a grip on many people. Pray that the power of God would break enemy strongholds over these temporary desires that seem so alluring.

Limited English proficiency is a challenge to residents seeking sustainable employment. Pray for churches to respond to this major opportunity for building relationships and sharing the gospel.

1 Perry, Marilyn Elizabeth. Hermosa. Encyclopedia of Chicago. http://encyclopedia.chicagohistory.org/pages/578.html.

# HUMBOLDT PARK

**AMOS 5:15**

*Hate evil, love good, and establish justice in the gate . . .*

## NEIGHBORHOODS

Humboldt Park

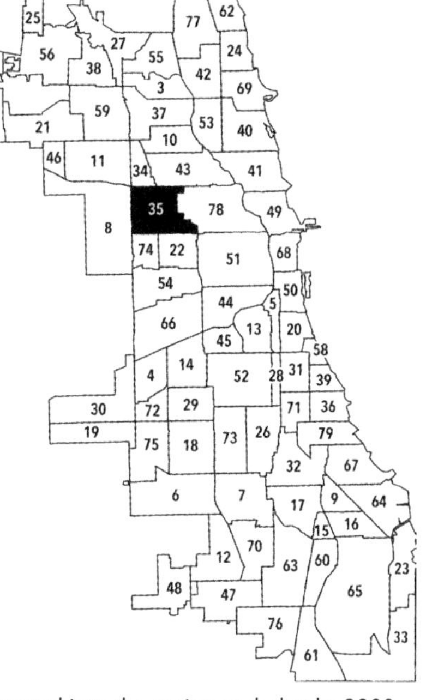


## DEMOGRAPHICS

Asian (0.4%), Black or African American (41.1%), Hispanic or Latino (52.5%), White (4.9%)

## LEARN

From its beginning, Humboldt Park has been a transient community, constantly experiencing changes in its ethnic population. In its earliest days, around the 1880s, the neighborhood was heavily Danish and Norwegian; the population changed as Germans, Scandinavians, and Poles settled into the area. Between the 1950s and 1960s, Puerto Ricans also migrated into the region. In June 1966, a three-day riot occurred when a policeman shot a young Puerto Rican man. These ethnic conflicts broiled during this transition period, which was heightened by the economic difficulties that many Puerto Ricans faced. The Division Street area, with its many stores and restaurants, has since become a permanent Puerto Rican community since the 1960s. During the 1980s, Mexicans moved into the region such that by 2000, 48 percent of Humboldt Park's population was Latino, half of which were of Mexican origin. At the same time, the black population also grew steadily to equal the size of the Latino population. More recently, Dominican immigrants have moved into the area, once again reflecting the constant changes in the community's rich ethnic population.[1]

## PRAY

Praise God for the discipleship that is taking place in the lives of young men in this community. Pray that the investment in these young men would have a ripple effect in the neighborhood as they stand up and grow in their walks with Christ.

Pray for families who have lost children due to gang violence. Pray that they would find support in the community and comfort from the Lord.

Pray for followers of Christ in the community who mourn with the troubled and who share the gospel throughout the neighborhood.

Pray against a large influence of witchcraft in this community, that it would not gain a deeper stronghold on the residents.

1 Badillo, David, A. Humboldt Park. Encyclopedia of Chicago. http://www.encyclopedia.chicagohistory.org/pages/617.html.

# ✓ HYDE PARK

**PHILIPPIANS 1:9**

*In this I pray, that your love may abound . . . in real knowledge and discernment.*

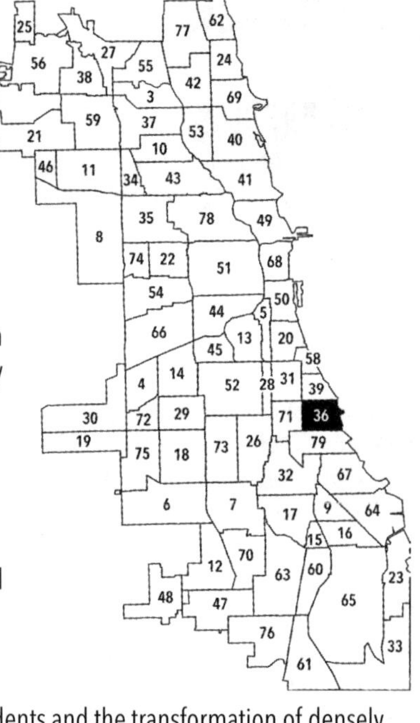


## NEIGHBORHOODS

Hyde Park

## DEMOGRAPHICS

Asian (11.1%), Black or African American (33.4%), Hispanic or Latino (5.3%), White (48.4%)

## LEARN

Hyde Park had modest growth and development until the founding of the University of Chicago and the World's Columbian Exposition of 1893. The popular Museum of Science and Industry still remains on this site. Building and development continued into the 1920s with prominent architects including Frank Lloyd Wright leading to diverse building structures and also increased diversity in the residents. By the early 1930s, Hyde Park was home to over one hundred hotels and many elaborate structures along the lakefront. However, concern later arose about increased crime and illegal residential conversion. As a result, the South East Chicago Commission was established in 1952 to counter local crime and monitor building code violations. The urban renewal plan was implemented resulting in many displaced residents and the transformation of densely built-up area to a "semi-suburbia." Hyde Park is considered to be a sought-after area with rich culture and architecture, and is home to the nationally acclaimed DuSable Museum of African American History.[1]

## PRAY

Hyde Park is experiencing renewed growth, leading to gentrification. Pray for those residents who are being displaced and for the assimilation of the residents with a long history in Hyde Park with new residents moving in.

The community spans a wide intellectual spectrum. Pray that Christians would be wisely visible and gently vocal as they engage meaningfully in Hyde Park from contacts on the streets to the halls of academia.

The University of Chicago attracts leaders from around the world. Pray for these students and the ministries reaching out to them, that they would experience Christ deeply and take Him with them as they return home.

✱Pray that the power of the gospel would penetrate and expose the shortcomings of political ideology, academic pride, and cultural liberalism.

1 Grinnell, Max. Hyde Park. Encyclopedia of Chicago. http://encyclopedia.chicagohistory.org/pages/622.html.

# IRVING PARK

**ISAIAH 1:17**

*Learn to do good, seek justice . . .*
*defend the orphan; plead for the widow.*

## NEIGHBORHOODS

Irving Park, Kilbourn Park, Old Irving Park, The Villa

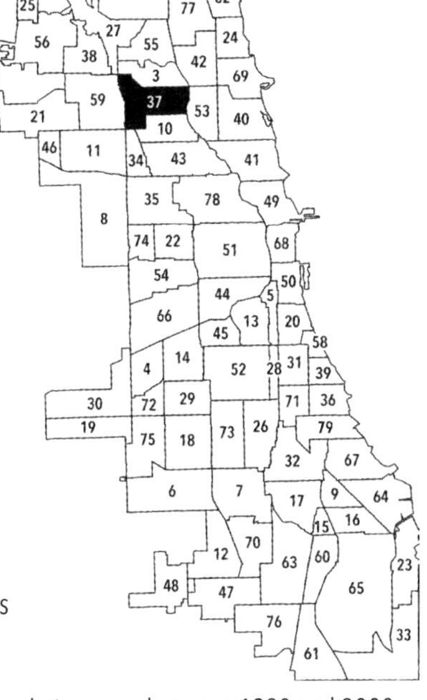


## DEMOGRAPHICS

Asian (7.2%), Black or African American (3.5%), Hispanic or Latino (44.3%), White (43.2%)

## LEARN

Irving Park began as a commuter suburb, with "shady streets, fine schools, churches and stores," attracting many rich and middle-class Protestants. Following annexation to Chicago in 1889, public transportation was established and streets were reconstructed, leading to an influx of new residents and a dramatic shift in housing composition. Well known for its past and present ties to preserving historic housing buildings, Irving Park neighborhoods are known for having notable architecture: the bungalows of the Villa District, Victorian and Italianate houses of Old Irving Park, and vintage homes in Independence Park. Two associations were formed in the 1980s for the preservation of neighborhood houses and notable landmarks. Irving Park's population grew between 1980 and 2000, but has since begun a slow decline. During that time, the Hispanic population grew from 9 percent to 46 percent, including immigrants from places throughout Central and South America.[1]

## PRAY

There has been a large influx of the Latino community in this area; many have struggled to find gainful employment. Pray for increased economic opportunities for these neighborhood residents.

Pray for a healthy interaction of cultures within the community, valuing and learning from each other, especially as the cultural demographic has changed dramatically.

Pray for the existing churches to find ways to creatively reach out to their neighbors and for an even greater increase of the body of Christ to serve the community.

Praise God for efforts within the community that are helping strengthen families and caring for their children within the foster care system.

1 Perry, Marilyn Elizabeth. Irving Park. Encyclopedia of Chicago. http://encyclopedia.chicagohistory.org/pages/655.html.

# JEFFERSON PARK

**NEHEMIAH 1:6**

*Let Thine ear be attentive and Thine eyes open to hear the prayer of Thy servant . . .*

## NEIGHBORHOODS

Gladstone Park, Jefferson Park

## DEMOGRAPHICS

Asian (6.9%), Black or African American (0.3%), Hispanic or Latino (19.9%), White (70.3%)

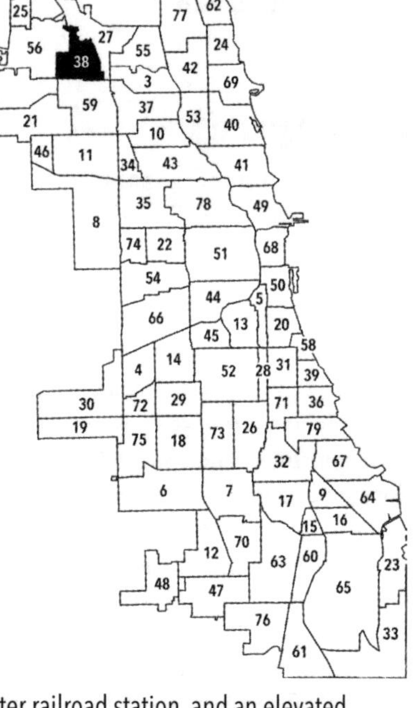


## LEARN

Jefferson Park has been called the "Gateway to Chicago" throughout its history. This identity was originally established in the 1800s when traders and hunters would transport goods in and out of Chicago and use Jefferson Park as a resting stop along the way. In the early 1900s, street railways were introduced into the neighborhood, bringing with it a flood of new residents. Against the desires of many residents, the neighborhood continued its role as the "Gateway to Chicago" in 1959 due to the construction of the Kennedy Expressway, which cut diagonally through Jefferson Park. Shortly after the construction of the Kennedy Expressway, the Chicago Transit Authority (CTA) built a terminal connecting CTA and Regional Transit Authority bus routes, a Greyhound bus stop, a Chicago & North Western commuter railroad station, and an elevated line. The area continues to attract many commuters with the Metra serving 10,000 a day and 800 buses traveling through Jefferson Park's main channels.[1]

## PRAY

Although a primarily white community, the neighborhood experiences more racial diversity each decade with more Latino and Asian Americans.

Pray for ongoing stability and a healthy interaction of cultures.

Jefferson Park is a large transportation hub. Pray for the thousands of people traveling through Jefferson Park each day, that they could come to know their Savior.

Post-modern religious influence is growing in the community, especially within the younger generation. Pray that the enemy would not use this movement as a foothold in this generation.

Jefferson Park is home to many aging Eastern Europeans. Pray that their heritage is remembered through generations and that these residents would not be overlooked by the churches in the area.

1 Perry, Marilyn Elizabeth. Jefferson Park. Encyclopedia of Chicago. http://www.encyclopedia.chicagohistory.org/pages/667.html.

# KENWOOD

**MATTHEW 23:23**

*Woe to you . . . you have neglected . . .
justice and mercy and faithfulness . . .*

## NEIGHBORHOODS

Kenwood

## DEMOGRAPHICS

Asian (5.5%), Black or African American (71.8%), Hispanic or Latino (2.9%), White (16.6%)

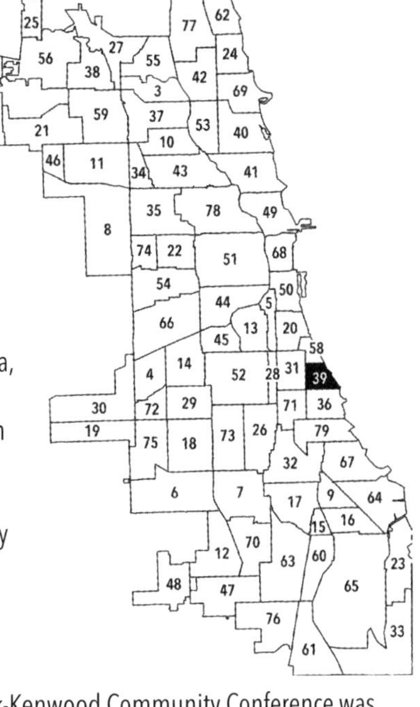


## LEARN

This area was first settled in the 1850s by inhabitants hoping to separate themselves from the hustle and bustle of downtown Chicago. Many of Chicago's prominent residents lived in the area, and the community continued to prosper through the 1890s. However, once the "L" reached Kenwood in 1907, the population increased greatly along with smaller living accommodations. The population continued to increase into the 1930s when the community was starting to show signs of deterioration and many existing apartments were subdivided. The transient community was moving either out of the area or into the northern part of community, while the southern part was populated with an influx of African Americans from the southern part of Chicago. To assist with the transitions in the neighborhood, the Hyde Park-Kenwood Community Conference was established in the late 1940s in order to maintain a stable and integrated neighborhood. Fortunately, Kenwood benefitted from the urban renewal funds from the Community Conference and the designation of historical districts and development of new residential construction. In the 1990s, the creation of charter schools also led many families to move back to the community.[1] Kenwood has recently received attention as the Chicago home of President Barack and Michelle Obama.

## PRAY

There has been a recent influx of young professionals into the neighborhood. Pray for cultural sensitivity and a healthy interaction with the community residents that have been there for a long time.

Kenwood is one of the communities affected by the Chicago Public School's restructuring with schools closing in this neighborhood. Pray for the children impacted by these decisions and needing to adapt to a different neighborhood.

Thank God for community organizations that are committed to the greater well-being of the neighborhood. Pray that God would bless the work they are doing in Kenwood.

1 Grinnell, Max. Kenwood. Encyclopedia of Chicago. http://encyclopedia.chicagohistory.org/pages/689.html.

# LAKE VIEW

**COLOSSIANS 3:14**

*And beyond all these things, put on love, which is the perfect bond of unity.*

## NEIGHBORHOODS

Boystown, Graceland West, Lake View, Lake View East, North Halsted, West Lake View, Wrigleyville

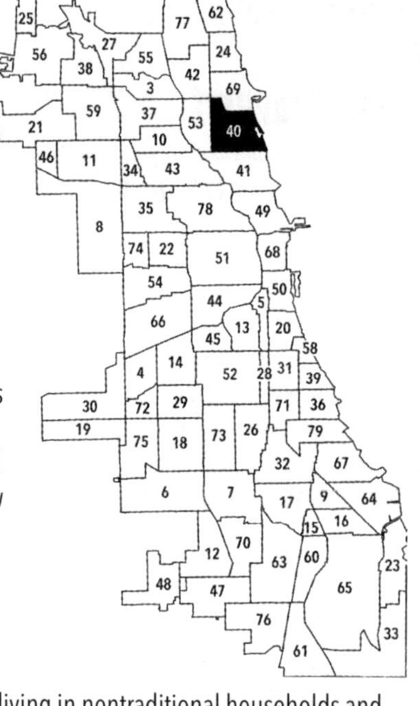

## DEMOGRAPHICS

Asian (6.0%), Black or African American (3.4%), Hispanic or Latino (8.0%), White (81.4%)

## LEARN

Lake View quickly became urbanized, welcoming new residents to its commercial and recreational facilities. To meet the demands of increased interest in the area, developers built high-rise apartment buildings and multiple-unit low-rises, which appealed to singles and young couples. Efforts were made by the Lake View Citizens Council in the 1950s to preserve the original heritage of the area. Despite these efforts, Lake View's residents were primarily single and young couples, with very few traditional families.[1] By the 1950s, the Lesbian Gay Bisexual Transgender (LGBT) community grew to be an identifiable population in Lake View's Boystown and by 1990, more than 22,000 residents were living in nontraditional households and were between the ages of twenty-five and forty-four. Today, Lake View is still widely known for its large population of nontraditional households.[2]

## PRAY

The neighborhood of Wrigleyville in Lake View draws many Cubs baseball fans to the bars and restaurants surrounding the ballpark. Pray for the gospel to be a more powerful force than the lure of the party scene.

Many of those in Boystown wrestling with same-sex attraction have experienced deep wounds from people who did not understand or who lacked in compassion. Pray for healing and openness to a Christ-centered gospel.

There are multiple churches and ministries in Lake View that seek to reach the numerous subcultures in the community, including runaways, homeless, and goth and punk cultures. Pray for creativity and perseverance of these ministries. Pray for a deep heart of compassion for all of us as Christ-followers to walk with the hurting in this community. Pray for tears of love and a gospel of reconciliation.

1 Seligman, Amanda. Lake View. Encyclopedia of Chicago. http://www.encyclopedia.chicagohistory.org/pages/715.html.

2 Gellman, Erick. Boystown. Encyclopedia of Chicago. http://www.encyclopedia.chicagohistory.org/pages/160.html.

# LINCOLN PARK

**EPHESIANS 6:18**

*With all prayer and petition pray at all times in the Spirit.*

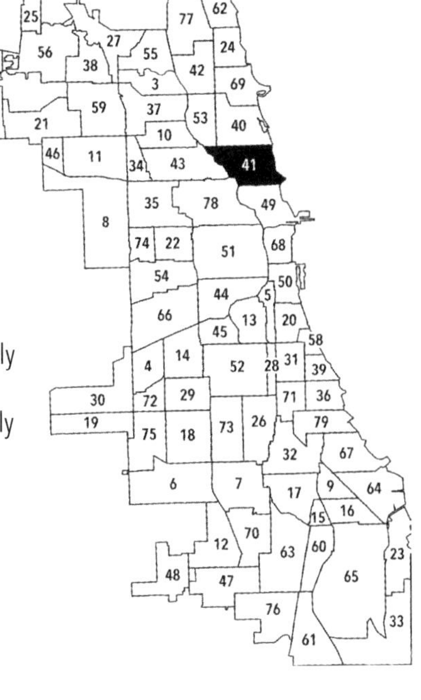


## NEIGHBORHOODS

Lincoln Park, Ranch Triangle

## DEMOGRAPHICS

Asian (5.5%), Black or African American (4.9%), Hispanic or Latino (5.1%), White (82.9%)

## LEARN

In the nineteenth century, Lincoln Park included affluent residents, industrial workers, and German farmers. In 1871, the area was greatly affected by the Great Chicago Fire, but eventually was rebuilt with many factories and repopulated with working-class residents. The eastern section remained populated primarily by middle-class and wealthy residents. By the early twentieth century, Lincoln Park was regarded as a firmly established residential area. DePaul University was established in 1898. However, like most other neighborhoods, Lincoln Park suffered from the Great Depression, but several initiatives renewed the area and, in the latter part of the twentieth century, land values increased dramatically. It is now one of the highest-status neighborhoods in Chicago.[1]

## PRAY

Lincoln Park is home to many young professionals, who have recently graduated from college. Pray for their transition into the workforce and that they could use their jobs for the glory of the Lord.

Pray for local elementary schools where efforts are being made to assist at-risk students. Pray that volunteers would be making an impact in the students' lives as well as blessing the school for Christ.

Pray for spiritual revival on DePaul's college campus located right in the middle of Lincoln Park. Pray for the effectiveness of the campus ministries reaching out to the student population.

Pray for the young men and women who live in a local residency that caters to the marginalized. Many do not know Christ and have very difficult life stories that have brought them to Chicago.

Pray for the senior living apartments in Lincoln Park. Pray that the men and women there would feel loved by their local churches and would place their trust in their Savior Jesus Christ.

1 Seligman, Amanda. Lincoln Park. Encyclopedia of Chicago. http://encyclopedia.chicagohistory.org/pages/746.html.

# LINCOLN SQUARE

**1 SAMUEL 1:27**

*For this . . . I prayed and the Lord has given me my petition . . .*

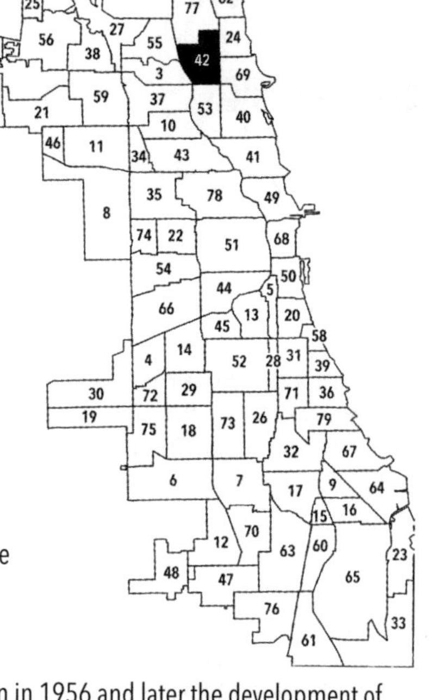


## NEIGHBORHOODS

Lincoln Square, Bowmanville, Ravenswood, Ravenswood Gardens

## DEMOGRAPHICS

Asian (13.0%), Black or African American (4.7%), Hispanic or Latino (18.6%), White (61.2%)

## LEARN

Lincoln Square began primarily in commercial agriculture through the 1800s. As transportation developed, new residents flooded into Lincoln Square. Among the new residents were many Greeks, whose small businesses set the groundwork for the "new Greektown" after the old Greektown had been displaced. Industries popped up along the North Western Railway tracks along Ravenswood Avenue, including Abbott Laboratories. Lincoln Square was soon known as Ravenswood due to its residential nature. However, in 1949, the Lincoln Square Chamber of Commerce began promoting a commercial image of the community. Empty storefronts and the lack of customers following WW II led to the erection of a statue of Abraham Lincoln in 1956 and later the development of the Lincoln Square mall in 1978. The empty storefronts eventually filled up with business owners of various ethnic backgrounds, including Latinos and Asians, who found the residential nature of Lincoln Square appealing.[1]

## PRAY

There has been a renewed interest in church planting in this community. Pray for the churches that are building relationships and sowing seeds and for their effectiveness in the community.

Former business establishments are being converted to lofts. Pray for the residents moving into the lofts to realize their need of the gospel.

Pray for the German culture within this area, that they would be reached for Christ and therefore influence their homeland for Christ as well. Pray for the efforts, which help fund, develop, and administer various programs aimed at improving the life of its residents.

Lincoln Square is home to many art schools, studios, and theaters. Pray that the gifts and talents of these musicians, artists, and actors would point to and draw people toward the glory of God.

1 Seligman, Amanda. Lincoln Square. Encyclopedia of Chicago. http://encyclopedia.chicagohistory.org/pages/747.html.

# LOGAN SQUARE

**PSALM 140:12**

*I know that the Lord will maintain . . . justice for the poor.*

## NEIGHBORHOODS

Bucktown, Logan Square, Palmer Square

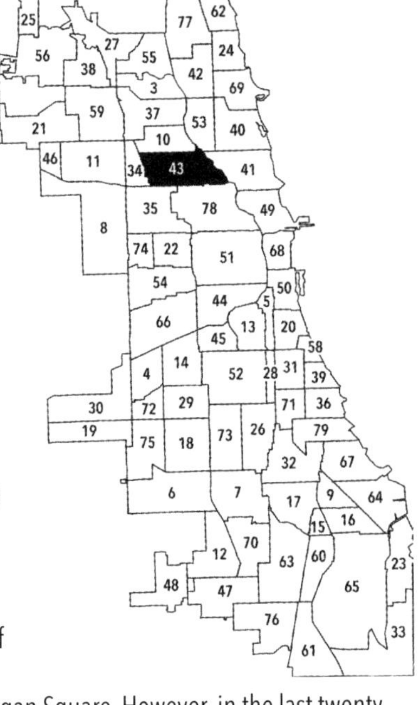


## DEMOGRAPHICS

Asian (3.1%), Black or African American (6.7%), Hispanic or Latino (53.5%), White (35.4%)

## LEARN

Logan Square remained undamaged during the Chicago Fire in 1871 and grew rapidly thereafter. German and Scandinavian immigrants moved in as the Milwaukee Avenue street railway was established. The construction of the "L" in 1890 led to the rapid building of new homes around the train stations and to developing a boulevard system. Following World War I, Logan Square boomed in population as Poles and Russian Jews moved into the area, leading to further construction of rental flats. After 1930, the population of Logan Square began to drop. The construction of the Northwest Expressway in the 1950s and the Blue Line disrupted commercial life, leading to the evacuation of most residents. Groups of Hispanic people moved into the area, and by 1990, made up almost two-thirds of the population of Logan Square. However, in the last twenty years, the area has seen major gentrification with a major growth in the white population and a decline in the Hispanic population by over 20 percent.[1]

## PRAY

Logan Square is experiencing major gentrification with affluent residents moving in and living next door to the less wealthy residents that previously occupied the area. Pray for sensitivity to and appreciation for the others' cultural identity.

Pray for churches to navigate through the processes of gentrification with wisdom and humility so that reconciliation can permeate the community.

Pray for the displaced people who have been residents in Logan Square for years. Pray for a smooth transition as they move to other neighborhoods and engage with schools and neighborhood services.

Pray for those who are interested and skilled in the arts and entertainment, that they would use these gifts for the greater good and benefit of the community.

1 Patterson, Elizabeth A. Logan Square. Encyclopedia of Chicago. http://www.encyclopedia.chicagohistory.org/pages/761.html.

# LOWER WEST SIDE

**MICAH 6:8**

*. . . do justice . . . love kindness . . .*
*walk humbly with your God.*

## NEIGHBORHOODS

Heart of Chicago, Lower West Side, Pilsen

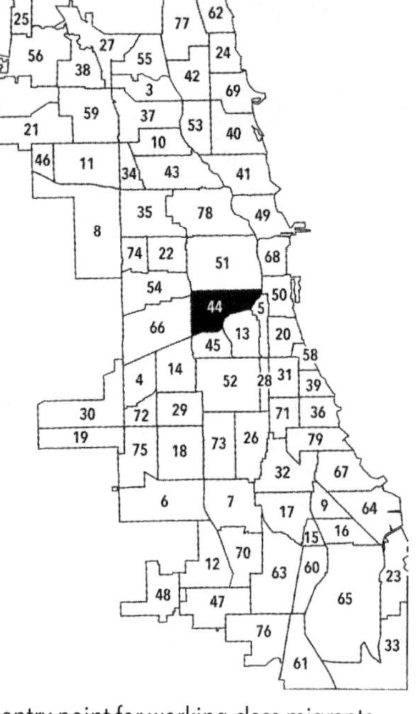


## DEMOGRAPHICS

Asian (0.5%), Black and African American (2.9%), Hispanic or Latino (81.8%), White (13.7%)

## LEARN

After the Chicago Fire of 1871, Pilsen became a center of manufacturing and a major industrial area. It was not until the hardships of the Great Depression and the housing crisis during World War II that the working-class area was strained by industries closing their plants. However, the urban renewal in the Near West Side along with the construction of the Stevenson Expressway helped to revitalize the area. Many Mexican residents moved farther south into Pilsen from the Near West Side with the convenience of the Stevenson Expressway followed by further immigration into Pilsen with the closing of the meatpacking plants and stockyard districts. Throughout the 1960s and 1970s, Mexicans from out of state, Puerto Ricans, and African Americans from North Lawndale also moved into the area. Pilsen remains an entry point for working-class migrants and is also home to the National Museum of Mexican Art. Many continue to struggle against poverty and discrimination as they receive help from mutual benefit societies.[1]

## PRAY

The Lower West Side is an entry point for many newcomers to the community. Pray that they become established in their community and are receptive to the gospel.

The population is predominantly Latino with strong ties to Mexico. Pray that others could embrace and remember their Mexican heritage.

There is a strong and influential arts community that is represented in the neighborhood, which has brought in a post-modern worldview. Pray that these artists could see that only Christ can meet their deepest longings.

There is an underrepresented evangelical church presence in the neighborhood. Pray for church planting efforts to engage the community.

1 Arrendondo, Gabriela F. Lower West Side. Encyclopedia of Chicago. http://www.encyclopedia.chicagohistory.org/pages/1174.html.

# MCKINLEY PARK

**EPHESIANS 2:10**

*For we are His workmanship, created . . . for good works . . .*

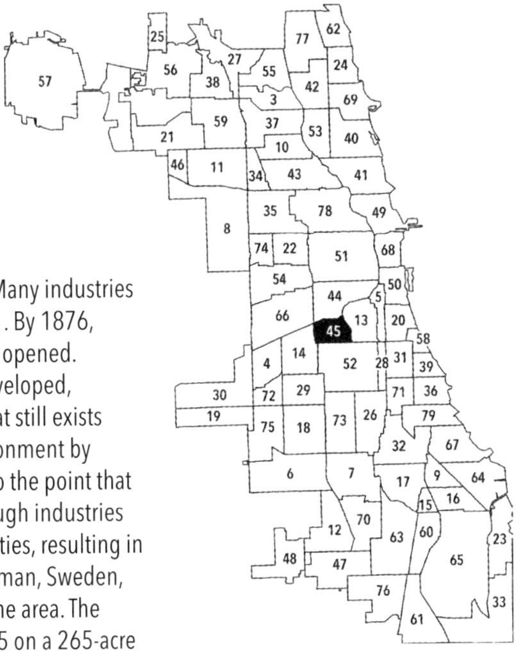

## NEIGHBORHOODS

McKinley Park

## DEMOGRAPHICS

Asian (13.2%), Black or African American (1.4%), Hispanic or Latino (61.1%). White (22.9%)

## LEARN

McKinley Park was annexed to Chicago in 1863. Many industries relocated to McKinley Park due to the Fire of 1871. By 1876, eleven new factories and twenty-seven brickyards opened. During this time meatpacking operations also developed, resulting in a strong working-class community that still exists to this day. The packinghouses polluted the environment by dumping wastes directly into the Chicago River, to the point that the river became known as "Bubbly Creek." Although industries created pollution, they also created job opportunities, resulting in population growth during the 1870s as Irish, German, Sweden, English, and native-born Americans moved into the area. The Central Manufacturing District was started in 1905 on a 265-acre industrial park. Other giant industries operated in this region, including Pepsi-Cola, the Wrigley Company, and the Chicago Sun-Times. At the beginning of the twentieth century, a 69-acre park was created that was named for President McKinley after his assassination, which has led to the naming of the entire community. In the 1990s, Mexicans moved into the area and new infill housing began to be built. The CTA rapid transit stations were built in the area, which has spurred development of shops and also increased property values.[1]

## PRAY

Pray for the churches that are looking to plant in this community, that they would be creative in their outreach efforts.

The neighborhood has many new and diverse residents. Pray that they would be united across racial lines.

Pray for this neighborhood's younger population, that the lure of gangs and drugs would be replaced by an authentic faith.

As the neighborhood continues to evolve, pray that the church would have a strong presence and be part of the glue that gives identity and vision to the area.

1 Solzman, David M. McKinley Park. Encyclopedia of Chicago. http://encyclopedia.chicagohistory.org/pages/802.html.

# MONTCLARE

**PSALM 10:14**

*Thou hast been the helper of the orphan.*

## NEIGHBORHOODS

Montclare

## DEMOGRAPHICS

Asian (1.4%), Black or African American (2.2%), Hispanic or Latino (55.5%), White (40.3%)

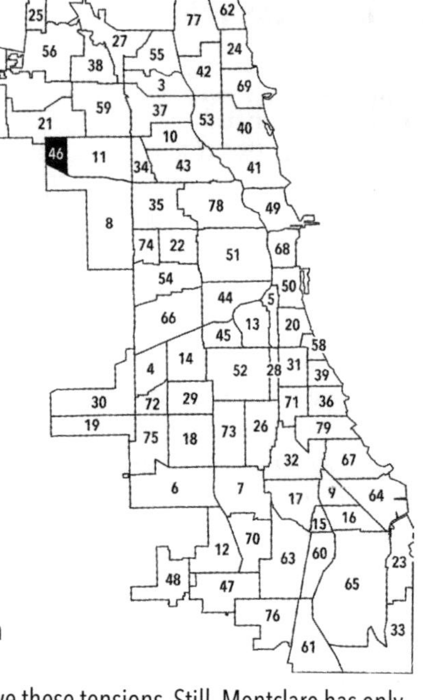


## LEARN

Montclare was established by William Sayre in 1836. Farmers in Montclare would take their produce to downtown markets in Chicago. In 1873, the Milwaukee & St. Paul Railroad poorly accommodated commuter transport into the area in the form of a single daily train. As a result, few settlers added to the tiny farming community of around 120 residents. Eventually, Montclare was annexed to Chicago in 1889. With the development of the Grand Avenue streetcar line, the first population growth spurt occurred. Single-family structures dominated the region, and Montclare continues to retain this suburban identity on Chicago's western side. In the late 1980s, a few African Americans moved into the neighborhood, which led to racial tension. Community organizations were formed to relieve these tensions. Still, Montclare has only a few African American residents, although the Hispanic population has grown to over 55 percent.[1]

## PRAY

The community is a strong mix of whites and Latinos on the edge of the Western suburbs. Pray for stability and compassionate interfacing of the two cultures.

Religious influence is not as predominant within the culture. Pray for churches to sensitively and creatively engage the community.

Community concerns revolve around the needs of the family, some of which are quite significant. Pray for the safety of the community, for wholesome activities for children, and for freedom from gang influence.

There are very limited employment opportunities for low-skilled workers. Pray for stable jobs and employment opportunities for workers to provide for their families.

1 Perry, Marilyn Elizabeth. Montclare. Encyclopedia of Chicago. http://encyclopedia.chicagohistory.org/pages/839.html.

# MORGAN PARK

**1 THESSALONIANS 5:15,17**

*. . . always seek after that which is good for one another . . . pray without ceasing.*

## NEIGHBORHOODS

Beverly Woods, Kennedy Park, Morgan Park, West Morgan Park

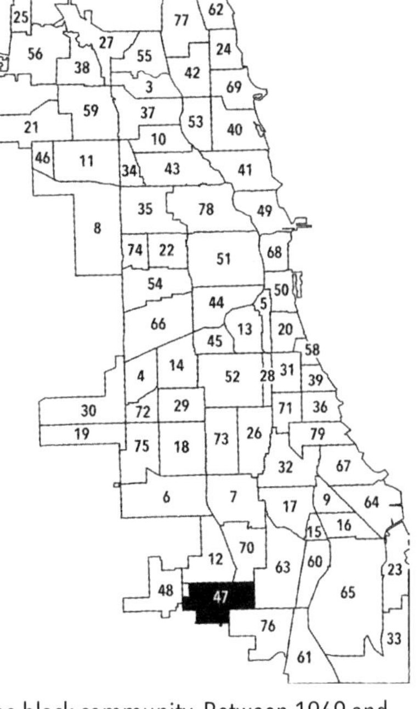


## DEMOGRAPHICS

Asian (1.1%), Black or African American (54.8%), Hispanic or Latino (5.4%), White (37.2%)

## LEARN

The middle-class status of Morgan Park was strengthened with the development of mainline Protestant churches that were established in the mid-1800s. Although Morgan Park became a prominently white Anglo-Saxon Protestant community, there was also a small settlement of African Americans living in the area, segregated to the east side of Vincennes. Although the number of African Americans living in Morgan Park continued to increase through 1920, the community was geographically divided. There was a "common understanding" that African Americans were not to live west of Vincennes Road. Racial integration did not begin to occur until the late 1960s, which was even more challenging due to the development of Interstate 57, which further isolated the black community. Between 1969 and 1974, four hundred "section 235" subsidized housing units were constructed. To this day, Morgan Park has worked to keep public schools integrated and shopping strips strengthened and is also home to the Walker Branch Library and the Beverly Arts Center.[1]

## PRAY

Female single-parent households are increasing in Morgan Park. Pray for access to resources for these families and positive male role models from within the community.

Pray for the many residents who have been recently displaced due to home foreclosures within the broader community.

There has been increased violence in neighborhood parks in the community. Pray that these places can be reclaimed for the enjoyment of the residents as they were originally intended.

Praise God for the numerous churches in this neighborhood. Pray that they would be united and work together to demonstrate the gospel in the community.

1 Skerrett, Ellen. Morgan Park. Encyclopedia of Chicago. http://encyclopedia.chicagohistory.org/pages/842.html.

# MOUNT GREENWOOD

**1 THESSALONIANS 1:2**

*We give thanks to God always for all of you, making mention of you in our prayers.*

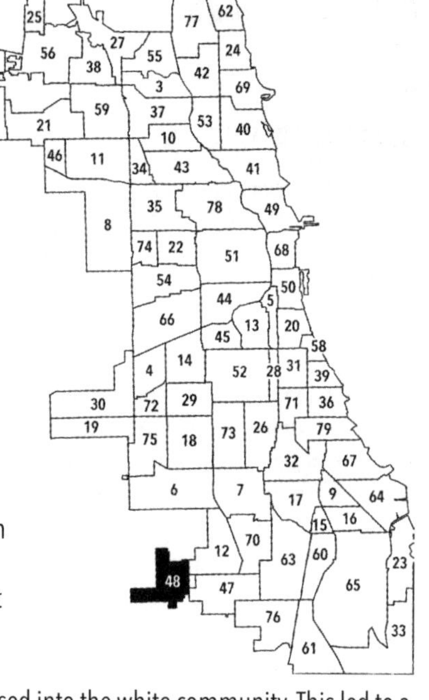

## NEIGHBORHOODS

Mount Greenwood, Talley's Corner

## DEMOGRAPHICS

Asian (0%), Black or African American (4.7%), Hispanic or Latino (5.8%), White (89.4%)

## LEARN

Mount Greenwood is bound by eight cemeteries and was once nicknamed the "Seven Holy Tombs." In 1897, taverns and restaurants opened to serve mourners after funerals. Mount Greenwood was annexed to Chicago in 1927 in hopes that this would catalyze improvements to the neighborhoods, such as the development of sewers, paved streets, and public schools. Such changes were slow to occur; however, in 1936, the sewage systems and paved and lighted streets were developed. Between 1930 and 1950, the population of Mount Greenwood grew rapidly. By 1980, Mount Greenwood contained the last farm that existed in Chicago; this was later developed into the Chicago High School for Agricultural Sciences. The magnet school stirred up controversy when, in the late 1980s, black students were bussed into the white community. This led to a community protest and racial hostility. Recently, the population has declined and became a densely white population, with African American and Hispanic populations still representing small percentages.[1]

## PRAY

This community is home to many of the police officers and firefighters who serve our city. Pray for their protection and praise God for these selfless individuals who sacrifice much for our city.

Mount Greenwood is a somewhat comfortable community, which often comes with complacency in seeking God. Pray that the residents would seek Christ instead of worldly things as sources of satisfaction and identity.

Because Mount Greenwood borders more underresourced communities, many youth visit, seeking entertainment. Pray that the church would see these as opportunities to reach out to the youth instead of regarding them as hindrances and troublemakers.

1 Stockwell, Clinton E. Mount Greenwood. Encyclopedia of Chicago. http://www.encyclopedia.chicagohistory.org/pages/848.html.

# NEAR NORTH SIDE

**2 CHRONICLES 7:14**

*[If] my people . . . humble themselves and pray and seek My face . . . then I will hear . . .*

## NEIGHBORHOODS

Cabrini-Green, The Gold Coast, Goose Island, Magnificent Mile, Near North Side, Old Town, River North, Streeterville

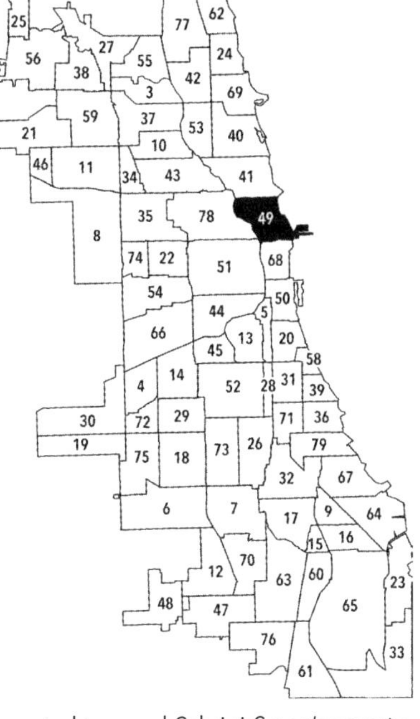


## DEMOGRAPHICS

Asian (8.2%), Black or African American (12.9%), Hispanic or Latino (5.1%), White (72.2%)

## LEARN

In the 1850s, wealthy residents developed the east side of the neighborhood with mansions, establishing Lake Shore Drive. The west side, on the other hand, became increasingly poor as an underresourced population was driven out of the east side. During the 1880s, the western area grew poorer and more disreputable as crime increased in the area. In the 1920s, the opening of the Michigan Avenue Bridge and the shopping area Magnificent Mile preserved the eastern region for the wealthy. This led to the construction of high-rise apartment buildings and luxury hotels. The imbalance of wealth in the Near North Side continued throughout the Great Depression. Housing officials attempted to mend Cabrini-Green's poverty by replacing the housing complexes with high-priced condos. Today, almost none of the original housing remains, and the area is encircled by expensive land, although many of its original residents, determined to stay in the neighborhood, remain.[1]

## PRAY

Pray that the existing division between social classes could be replaced with unity and service. The neighborhoods are phenomenally segregated along many lines, particularly financial.

Many in the community are primarily concerned with pursuing worldly success and fortune. Pray that God would change their focus to eternal kingdom values.

Many residents in the Gold Coast live a fast-paced lifestyle. Pray that people in the church would find time to dedicate their specific passions and giftings to be a positive influence in their community, workplaces, and families.

Pray for the people who have been displaced by gentrification in the neighborhood to be treated with dignity and respect and to find adequate housing for their families.

1 Arredondo, Gabriela F. Near North Side. Encyclopedia of Chicago. http://www.encyclopedia.chicagohistory.org/pages/876.html.

# NEAR SOUTH SIDE

**JONAH 4:11**

*. . . should I not have compassion on Nineveh, the great city . . .*

## NEIGHBORHOODS

Central Station, Dearborn Park, Museum Campus, Near South Side, Prairie Avenue Historic District, South Loop

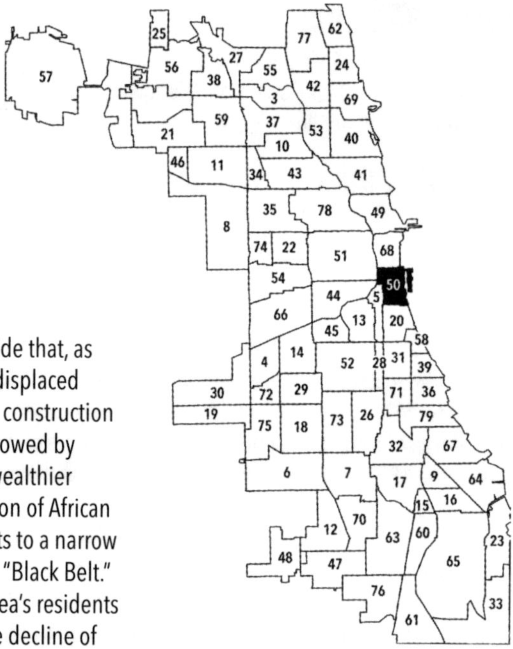

## DEMOGRAPHICS

Asian (12.9%), Black or African American (36.9%), Hispanic or Latino (4.8%), White (43.4%)

## LEARN

The Fire of 1871 did not extend into Near South Side that, as a result, became the temporary quarters of many displaced businesses. Rapid transit was established with the construction of the Elevated Railroad in the 1890s. This was followed by apartment and hotel building and the exodus of wealthier residents. Discrimination during the Great Migration of African Americans to Chicago confined these new residents to a narrow corridor on Chicago's South Side referred to as the "Black Belt." By the end of the twentieth century, most of the area's residents lived in Chicago Housing Authority complexes. The decline of passenger trains also left rail yards vacant. However, during the 1920s, notable redevelopment took place in the district's edges with the construction of parks and museums. Residential growth in the South Loop also extended into the Near South Side, making areas into residential streets once again after a century.[1]

## PRAY

Many commuter students come in and out of the Near South Side to study, due to the many universities represented in the area, such as Columbia College, East West University, and Harold Washington College. Pray for an effective ministry to the student population by the churches and parachurch groups.

Pray for better and more schools. School enrollment continues to increase and a long-term plan is desperately needed. Expansion in the South Loop is difficult due to little property available. Pray for better and more schools.

Every day, thousands of people move through the Roosevelt CTA stop, among which include both the affluent and the poor of Chicago. Pray for peace and justice to flow through the neighborhood.

1 McClendon, Dennis. Near South Side. Encyclopedia of Chicago. http://www.encyclopedia.chicagohistory.org/pages/877.html.

# NEAR WEST SIDE

**PSALM 133:1**

*Behold how good and how pleasant it is for brothers to dwell together in unity.*

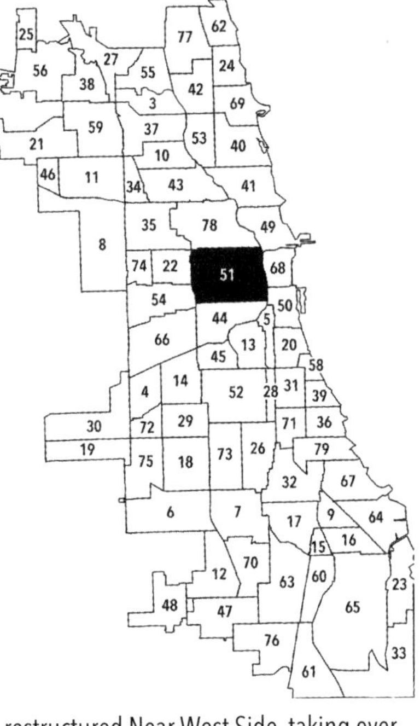


## NEIGHBORHOODS

Fulton River District, Greektown, Little Italy, Medical Center, Tri-Taylor, University Village

## DEMOGRAPHICS

Asian (11.7%), Black or African American (40.2%), Hispanic or Latino (7.2%), White (38.4%)

## LEARN

After the Fire of 1871, Near West Side became overcrowded with the 200,000 people who took refuge in the area. This brought many cultures into the neighborhood, including a settlement of Greeks in an area now known as Greektown. In the 1930s and 1940s, African Americans and Mexicans came in great numbers from the south to the urban north. The construction of the University of Illinois at Chicago also brought an end to much of the historic Italian neighborhood. In the 1950s and 1960s, the area was experiencing an increase in poverty and economic decline and was impacted even more by the riots following the assassination of Martin Luther King, Jr. in 1968. Toward the end of the twentieth century, the growth of the University once again restructured Near West Side, taking over the historical Maxwell Street Market. With this expansion, the area has more recently become a dwelling place for many middle- and upper-class residents who had interest in living near downtown.[1]

## PRAY

Greektown is an integral part of the community. Pray for a clear understanding of who Jesus is within the culture.

Little Italy is still a presence in the neighborhood despite some displacement. Pray for the maintenance of their cultural heritage and identity.

Thousands of students studying at University of Illinois-Chicago are in the neighborhood. Pray for the many campus ministries reaching out to the young people searching for meaning in life.

Near West Side houses a strong medical center that serves hundreds of people facing serious physical challenges and dealing with grief and anxiety. Pray for the caregivers, the patients, and their families, and the chaplains who minister to them.

1 Pauillac, Myriam. Near West Side. Encyclopedia of Chicago. http://www.encyclopedia.chicagohistory.org/pages/878.html.

# NEW CITY

**ZECH. 7:9,10**

*. . . practice kindness . . . do not oppress the widow . . . orphan . . . stranger . . . poor . . .*

## NEIGHBORHOODS

Back of the Yards, Canaryville, New City

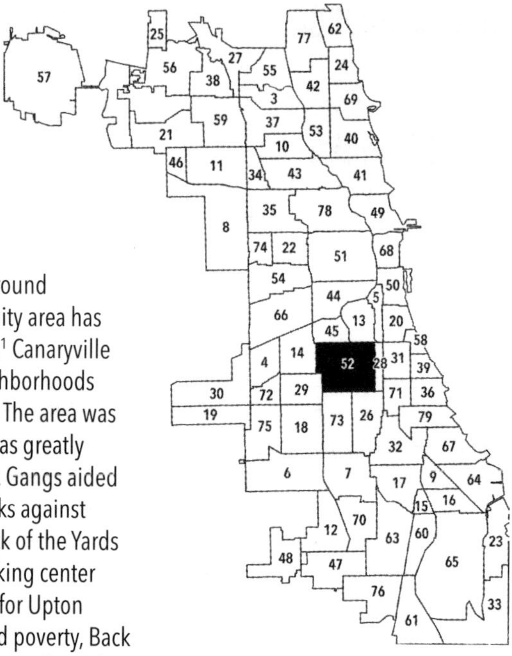

## DEMOGRAPHICS

Asian (1.0%), Black or African-American (31.5%), Hispanic or Latino (53.2%), White (13.3%)

## LEARN

New City's boundaries were drawn in the 1920s around Chicago's stockyards. However, this large community area has never embodied a cohesive culture or community.[1] Canaryville gained the reputation as one of the toughest neighborhoods in the city through much of the twentieth century. The area was largely populated by Irish, and the environment was greatly shaped by the stockyards and meatpacking center. Gangs aided in Canaryville's reputation and were active in attacks against African Americans during the 1919 Race Riot.[2] Back of the Yards contained the largest livestock yards and meatpacking center in the country until the 1950s. While most known for Upton Sinclair's *The Jungle,* and its pollution, squalor, and poverty, Back of the Yards also represented a strong and cohesive working-class community that organized itself through social and labor movements. However, with the ending of the meatpacking industry in the 1960s, the neighborhood has once again had to work through physical and economic deterioration with the hopes of the new manufacturing development.[3]

## PRAY

The departure of a large manufacturing industry has left a deep economic gap in the community. Pray for an infusion of jobs and stronger livelihood for neighborhood residents.

Filling the economic void has been a strong gang presence and pockets of violence resulting in multiple shootings. Pray for peace, safety, and a decrease in violence in the area.

New City has experienced great turbulence in local Chicago Public Schools as students are moved around because of recent school closings. Pray for the children who are affected and the educators seeking to teach them. An atmosphere of blight and discouragement permeates a once vibrant community. Pray for a spirit of hope and for spiritual and economic renewal.

1 Gellman, Erik. New City. Encyclopedia of Chicago. http://encyclopedia.chicagohistory.org/pages/882.html.

2 Barrett, James R. Canaryville. Encyclopedia of Chicago. http://www.encyclopedia.chicagohistory.org/pages/2476.html.

3 Barrett, James R. Back of the Yards. Encyclopedia of Chicago. http://www.encyclopedia.chicagohistory.org/pages/99.html.

# NORTH CENTER

**ACTS 11:26**

*. . . the disciples were first called Christians in Antioch.*

## NEIGHBORHOODS

North Center, Roscoe Village, Saint Ben's

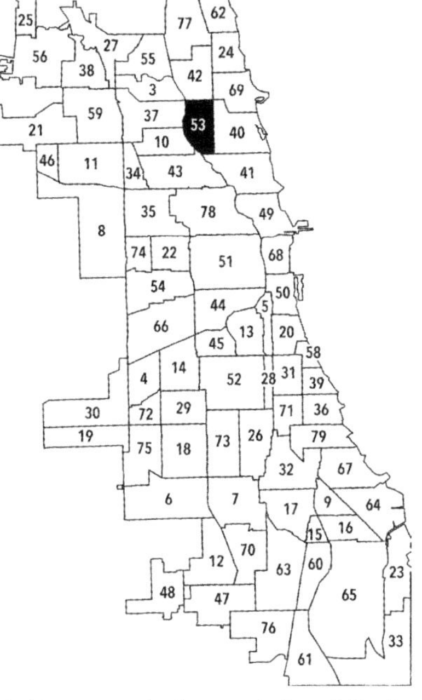


## DEMOGRAPHICS

Asian (3.9%), Black or African American (2.3%), Hispanic or Latino (13.3%), White (78.0%)

## LEARN

North Center's position by the North Branch of the Chicago River has played a big part of the history and settlement of the neighborhood. Concern from the Fire of 1871 led to a growth in the manufacturing of bricks near the river in North Center, earning the name Bricktown. Laborers in this industry moved to the working-class residential area. However, the construction of the "L" brought residents whose economic sustenance did not depend on local industry to settle in the area. The new residents disliked the unappealing sight of the clay pits. Eventually the clay pits shut down and unfortunately transformed into garbage pits ill-suited for residential development. During the Great Depression, one of Chicago's first public housing complexes was later developed in North Center, near the boundary to Lincoln Park. More recently, the population of North Center has decreased and been replaced with a diverse mix of Korean, Hispanic, and Filipino residents. Today, North Center comprises quaint modest homes and small businesses.[1]

## PRAY

North Center has a strong historical allegiance to a large and influential Catholic church in the community but is becoming increasingly de-churched and secular with many new residents also moving to the area. Pray for the opportunities to reach these people.

There has been a recent emphasis of evangelical churches to reengage in the neighborhood, by strengthening of existing churches and new church plants. Pray for receptivity and relevance of the gospel message.

North Center has a large number of singles with interest in music, the arts, and for social justice. Pray that the church would engage them with practical acts of service.

1 Seligman, Amanda. Lincoln Square.Encyclopedia of Chicago. http://encyclopedia.chicagohistory.org/pages/747.html.

# NORTH LAWNDALE

**EZEKIEL 22:30**

*I searched for a man among them who would build up the wall . . .*

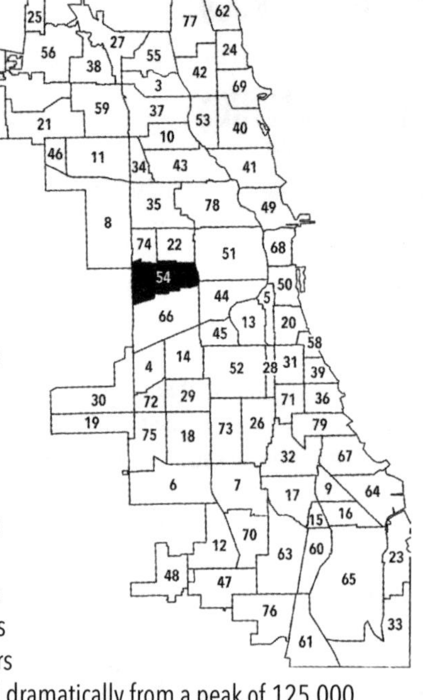


## NEIGHBORHOODS

Homan Square, K-Town, North Lawndale

## DEMOGRAPHICS

Asian (0.5%), Black or African American (91.3%), Hispanic or Latino (5.5%), White (1.8%)

## LEARN

Historically, North Lawndale was a home for Jewish refugees following the Great Fire of 1871 and continued to grow as factories moved into the area. In the early 1950s, the population changed drastically with a new influx of African American residents, many displaced from the urban renewal projects that took place in other neighborhoods in Chicago. No new housing was built during the time of increased population, employment was scarce, and the physical deterioration of the community was severe. Dr. Martin Luther King, Jr. chose North Lawndale as the base for his civil rights movement in Chicago. Unfortunately, the riots that followed King's assassination frightened factory owners and working residents to flee the area, including the former Sears headquarters. By the year 2000, Lawndale's population dropped dramatically from a peak of 125,000 to about 47,200; many residents left due to increased poverty, crime, and unemployment. However, glimmers of change exist today as many are working toward the betterment of North Lawndale.[1]

## PRAY

The neighborhood has never fully rebounded from the drastic loss of resources as industry left the community. Pray for a reinfusion of infrastructure and opportunity to energize the neighborhood.

Pray for underperforming schools that are reeling under the harsh reality of low expectations and few role models of success. Pray for the children, their parents, teachers, and staff to persevere despite the odds.

Pray for peace in North Lawndale's streets. Pray that churches and Christians in North Lawndale would be an active presence in the lives of their neighbors.

Praise the Lord for His servants who are providing services to meet the wide-ranging needs of the community including spiritual, social, medical, legal, and residential.

1 Seligman, Amanda. North Lawndale. Encyclopedia of Chicago. http://www.encyclopedia.chicagohistory.org/pages/901.html.

# NORTH PARK

**PSALM 122:6**

*Pray for the peace of Jerusalem, may they prosper who love you.*

## NEIGHBORHOODS

Hollywood Park, North Park, Peterson Park

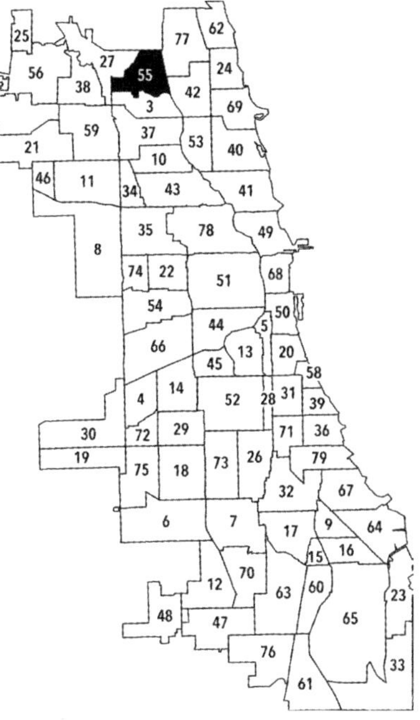


## DEMOGRAPHICS

Asian (27.7%), Black or African American (2.0%), Hispanic or Latino (16.1%), White (50.6%)

## LEARN

North Park has had a somewhat stable history of gradual growth and development. The area was originally settled by German and Swedish farmers and developed into a residential area between 1920 and 1930. The population grew even more after World War II and was stable due to the Covenant Hospital and other educational and civic institutions that still exist today. The area is considered somewhat unique in its unusual ambience created by streams and a nature preserve. North Park continues to be a stable and quiet neighborhood that is occupied by mostly middle-income residents.[1]

## PRAY

Praise God for the stability of this community and for the countless neighborhood families that benefit from Peterson Park, which is located in North Park.

Pray that, beyond the physical stability and security of the community, the spiritual climate would likewise be strong and influential.

Pray for the students, staff, and faculty of North Park College and Seminary, that they would have a positive influence on the community.

Pray for the numerous churches that are seeking to reach the community. Pray for unity, creative outreach, and for the perseverance to continue strong in ministry.

1 Solzman, David M. North Park. Encyclopedia of Chicago. http://www.encyclopedia.chicagohistory.org/pages/902.html.

# NORWOOD PARK

**MATTHEW 21:22**

*And all things you ask in prayer, believing, you shall receive.*

## NEIGHBORHOODS

Big Oaks, Norwood Park, Old Norwood, Oriole Park, Union Ridge

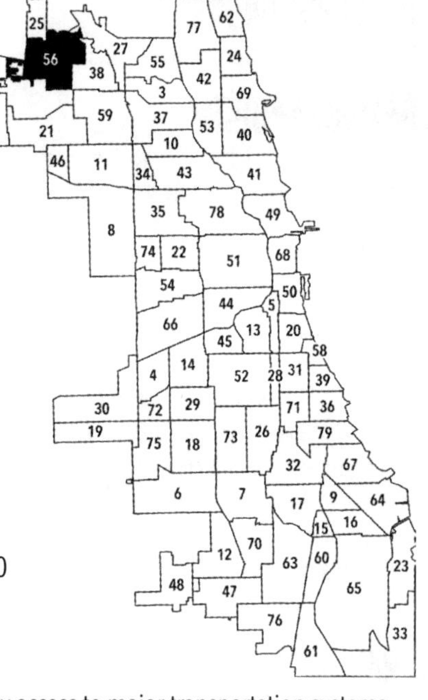


## DEMOGRAPHICS

Asian (4.9%), Black or African American (0.4%), Hispanic or Latino (13.5%), White (80.5%)

## LEARN

Early developers hoped to form Norwood Park into a resort, due to the area woodlands and hills. The subdivision of Norwood Park is curvilinear, rather than following the typical grid pattern. In the 1830s, English farmers settled in the area. Over the years, German immigrants moved in, along with Poles and Scandinavians. In 1893, Norwood Park was annexed to Chicago. Nine train stops were built to help residents commute into the city, and most homes were built near the railroad. Between 1970 and 2000, the population of Norwood Park began to decline. Housing types vary between Victorian houses to bungalows, ranches, and condominiums. Retail businesses line the Northwestern Highway, and residents of Norwood Park have easy access to major transportation systems, such as O'Hare Airport and trains. To this day, Norwood Park remains mostly residential in nature.[1]

## PRAY

Thank the Lord for the economic stability in this community.

Pray for the churches in this community to express a consistent and caring gospel witness to the residents in Norwood Park.

Pray for the established cultures within the community to sense their need for a personal relationship with Jesus Christ.

Praise the Lord for the preservation of a strong neighborhood identity. Pray also for an openness toward the newer, incoming residents.

1 Perry, Marilyn Elizabeth. Norwood Park. Encyclopedia of Chicago. http://www.encyclopedia.chicagohistory.org/pages/912.html.

# O'HARE

**JAMES 5:16**

*. . . The effective prayer of a righteous man can accomplish much.*

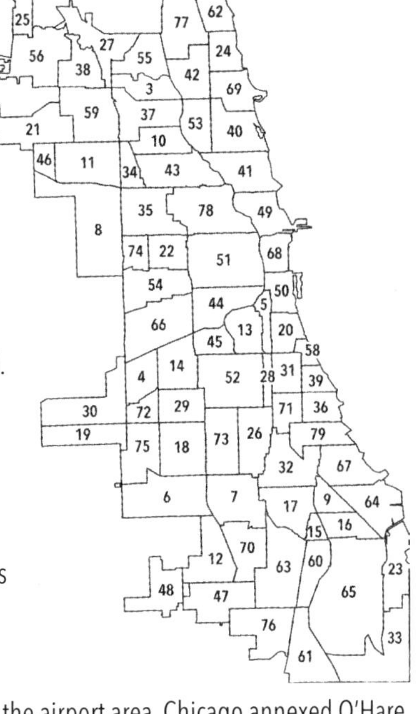


## NEIGHBORHOODS

O'Hare, Schorsch Forest View

## DEMOGRAPHICS

Asian (6.9%), Black or African American (0.9%), Hispanic or Latino (16.2%), White (75.4%)

## LEARN

O'Hare remained largely undeveloped prior to World War II. During the early 1840s, few families and immigrants from Germany settled in what would eventually become Higgins Road. In 1887, a depot along the Wisconsin Central Railroad opened in Orchard Place, an unincorporated area in the northeastern section of O'Hare. Despite the railroad, very few people settled in Orchard Place, and residential subdivisions that were built in the 1930s all but vanished after World War II. In 1942, Douglas Aircraft took over Orchard Place for the production of cargo planes during World War II. The facility then became a commercial airport. In 1947, the Chicago City Council picked Orchard Place as the location for the new international airport for Chicago and local facilities in the area were removed. To establish control over the airport area, Chicago annexed O'Hare in March 1956. The accelerated success of the airport precipitated the increase in neighboring land values.[1]

## PRAY

There is a large Polish community with a rich heritage. Pray that the evangelistic church will be sensitive to their culture when addressing this community.

The Des Plaines River cuts through O'Hare, and often incurs detrimental flooding in the area. Pray for the protection over the homes of residents.

Pray for the safety of community residents, as O'Hare is home to one of the busiest airports in the nation. Pray that the chapel services held at the airport will lead to the salvation of many travelers.

Chicago is a hub for human trafficking due to the international flights. Pray for laws to be passed to protect victims and prosecute perpetrators and for the release of slaves.

1 Seligman, Amanda. O'Hare. Encyclopedia of Chicago. http://encyclopedia.chicagohistory.org/pages/924.html.

# OAKLAND

**MATTHEW 5:44**

*But I say to you love your enemies and pray for those who persecute you.*

## NEIGHBORHOODS

Oakland

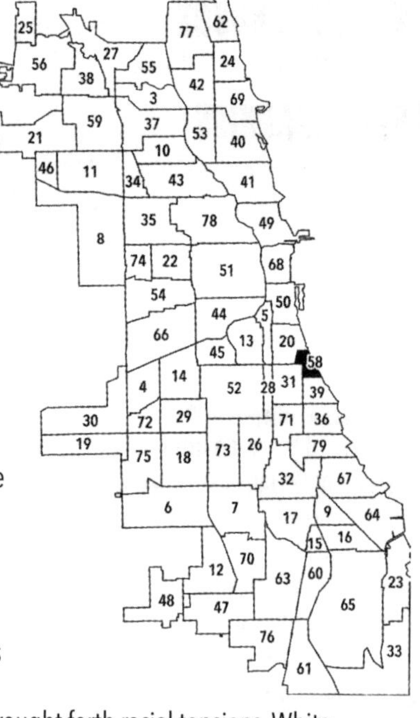


## DEMOGRAPHICS

Asian (0.9%), Black or African American (91.0%), Hispanic or Latino (2.7%), White (3.2%)

## LEARN

In 1851, Charles Cleaver built a soap factory in what is now known as Oakland, and the town began to boom with industry and was prosperous for many. Soon after, many residents flocked to the area because of the convenient location of stockyards and improved access to the city via the newly installed horsecar line. In 1871, real estate developers gave this neighborhood the name Oakland. The center of all the hustle and bustle in Oakland was a commercial district that later became known as Five Crossings, where the new residents, many who were affluent, came to shop. Between 1916 and 1920, many African Americans settled in Oakland during the Great Migration. The Oakland population was a diverse mixture of African Americans, Germans, Jews, English, Irish, and Japanese. An increasing African American population brought forth racial tensions. White residents resorted to violence and restrictive covenants to keep blacks from moving into Oakland, without success. By 1950, Oakland was 77 percent African American. After public housing projects were placed in Oakland in the 1970s, the streets of Oakland became crime-infested. Oakland even became home to the infamous El Rukn street gang. The neighborhood has remained below poverty level ever since.[1]

## PRAY

Praise God for the rich history of the African American community and the legacy of churches and institutions that shaped and preserved the culture.

Pray for the economic well-being of this community as more businesses are looking to establish a presence in the neighborhood. Pray that these businesses could provide employment to Oakland residents.

Pray that the youth in the community have opportunities to express their energy and youthfulness in productive ways rather than violence.

1 Tolson, Claudette. Oakland. Encyclopedia of Chicago. http://encyclopedia.chicagohistory.org/pages/919.html.

# PORTAGE PARK

**JEREMIAH 9:24**

*. . . I am the Lord who exercises loving kindness, justice, and righteousness on earth . . .*

## NEIGHBORHOODS

Portage Park

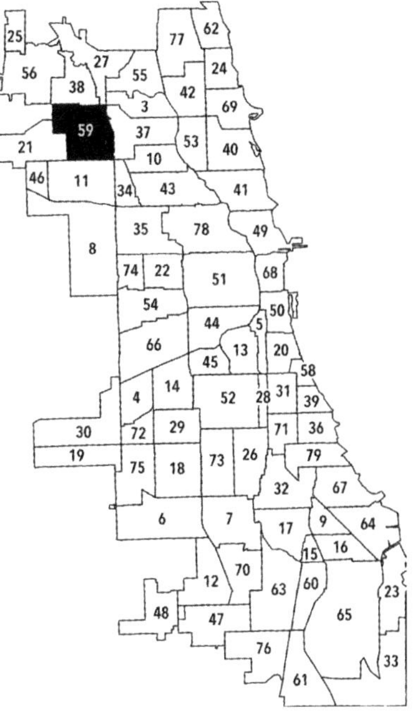


## DEMOGRAPHICS

Asian (5.2%), Black or African American (1.5%), Hispanic or Latino (34.5%), White (56.4%)

## LEARN

In 1912 residents in the area formed the Portage Park district; in the following year, forty acres of land were established for the purpose of a park construction. The park officially opened in 1916 with events organized by the Portage Park Citizens' Celebration Association. The park became a hubbub of recreational activities and included a swimming lagoon, tennis courts, and baseball fields. As transportation improved throughout the city, the park neighborhood became a popular place to move to such that, by 1940, the population of Portage Park rose to 66,357. Community activities continue to center on the park over the years. By 1990, the population decreased to 56,513 and was composed mostly of Polish, Irish, Italians, and Germans. To this day, many social activities and athletic events are centered at the Park.[1]

## PRAY

Pray for the development of ministries and organizations that focus on building up families. There are many young parents who reside in Portage Park. There is a need to train these young couples in parental skills and youth development.

Although the neighborhood population has been increasing, many homes have been foreclosed on in previous years creating overcrowding in multifamily homes. Pray for peace as the neighborhood continues to populate.

Pray for economic stability and growth in Portage Park. Many storefront businesses have closed down, resulting in a state of decline for those remaining.

Although Portage Park is a very diverse neighborhood, there is little violence and tension due to ethnic differences. Praise God for the relative peace that the residents experience.

1 Perry, Mary Elizabeth. Portage Park. Encyclopedia of Chicago. http://encyclopedia.chicagohistory.org/pages/994.html.

# PULLMAN

**ISAIAH 41:17**

*. . . the afflicted and needy are seeking water . . .*
*their tongue is parched with thirst . . .*

## NEIGHBORHOODS

Cottage Grove Heights, Pullman

## DEMOGRAPHICS

Asian (0%), Black or African American (83.4%), Hispanic or Latino (8.1%), White (8.4%)

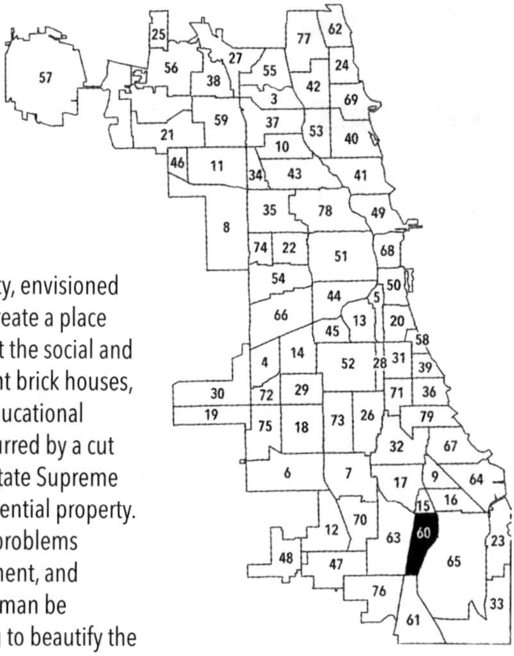

## LEARN

At its founding, Pullman was a planned community, envisioned and built by George M. Pullman in the 1870s to create a place for his new factory. He built an entire town to meet the social and physical health needs of his employees. This meant brick houses, access to schools, parks, a library, a theater, and educational programs. However, following a strike in 1894 spurred by a cut in wages without a decrease in rents, the Illinois State Supreme Court ordered the company to divest itself of residential property. Pullman was then annexed to Chicago, but faced problems of old housing, vacant industrial land, unemployment, and bootlegging. When it was recommended that Pullman be demolished, the residents fought back, organizing to beautify the neighborhood and founding the Historic Pullman Foundation in 1973. Pullman still retains much of its original architecture and spatial orientation. It attracts thousands of visitors each year. However, in recent decades it has seen a decline in housing and job opportunities and is now a hybrid of a lower-middle class neighborhood and a preserved historical district.[1]

## PRAY

Praise God for several ministries in the community that have represented Christ in caring, holistic outreach for those in need.

Pray for sensitivity to the historic landmarks within the community to preserve a unique legacy that contributed to the greater identity of the South Side of Chicago.

Praise God for newer economic developments that are bringing employment opportunities to the residents of Pullman. Pray that the previously established businesses would benefit from the renewed focus.

There is a local hospital in a strategic position to benefit the community. Pray that it would acquire the proper resources and that the quality of care would meet the deepest needs of the community.

1 Reiff, Janice L. Pullman. Encyclopedia of Chicago. http://www.encyclopedia.chicagohistory.org/pages/1030.html.

# RIVERDALE

**HEBREWS 11:16**

*He has prepared a city for them.*

## NEIGHBORHOODS

Altgeld Gardens, Eden Green, Golden Gate

## DEMOGRAPHICS

Asian (1.2%), Black or African American (97.7%), Hispanic or Latino (0.6%), White (0.5%)

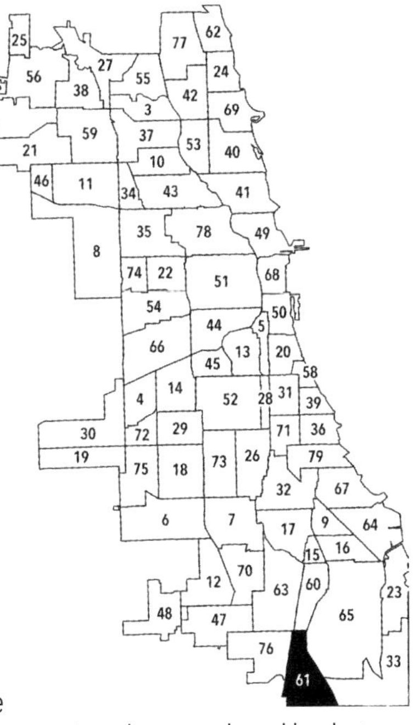


## LEARN

The former swampland of Riverdale was later used for industrial and manufacturing purposes, with its largest industry being Calumet Paint. In the early 1900s, Sherwin-Williams purchased this plant and the rest is history. It went on to become one of the largest paint manufacturers in America. With this new industrialism, Riverdale provided jobs not only to its citizens, but to those living in other areas of Chicago as well. However, Riverdale was not exempt from hardship. Government actions transitioned Riverdale from an industrial to a residential area by opening a massive housing project called Altgeld Gardens in 1945. The swift transformation of the area led from a population of 1,500 in the 1940s to 12,000 by the 1960s and a racially tense battleground among schools, hospitals, and business. Riverdale has continued to struggle and has lost both jobs and population. By 1990, 63 percent of households lived below the poverty level and 35 percent of workers were unemployed.[1]

## PRAY

The living conditions in Riverdale are adversely affected by the landfill and water sewage treatment plant. Pray for the health of the community residents.

Fighting among gangs and the influence of drugs are scarring the community. Pray that local ministries would be a beacon of light to the children and teenagers in the neighborhood.

Pray for the churches that are seeking to strategically and spiritually recalibrate vacant industrial property for kingdom purposes.

There is tension and rivalry between local high schools that has escalated at times to violence. Pray for peace among the students and wisdom and endurance for teachers and administrators.

1 Reiff, Janice L. Riverdale. Encyclopedia of Chicago. http://encyclopedia.chicagohistory.org/pages/1077.html.

# ROGERS PARK

**JUDE 20:21**

*But you beloved . . . praying in the Holy Spirit; keep yourselves in the love of God . . .*

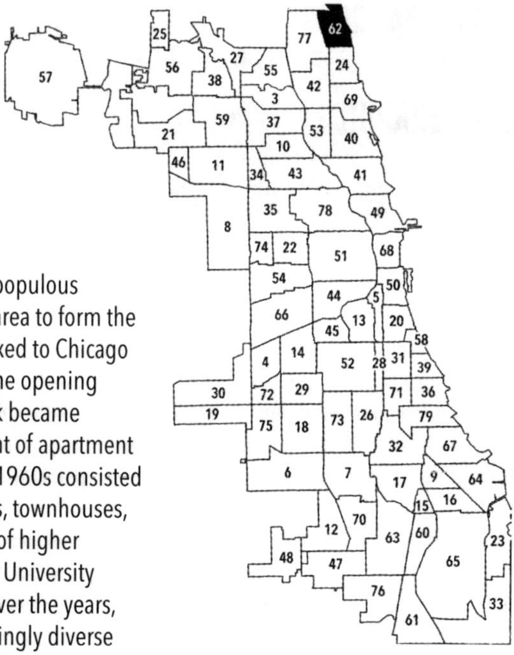

## NEIGHBORHOODS

Loyola, Rogers Park

## DEMOGRAPHICS

Asian (6.4%), Black or African American (26.4%), Hispanic or Latino (25.7%), White (38.2%)

## LEARN

Rogers Park is one of Chicago's most diverse and populous neighborhoods. In 1878, settlers moved into the area to form the village of Rogers Park, which was eventually annexed to Chicago in 1893. The population jumped drastically with the opening of Howard Station along the "L" tracks. Rogers Park became primarily home to renters due to the establishment of apartment complexes in the region. New construction in the 1960s consisted primarily of moderately sized apartment buildings, townhouses, and nursing homes. Additionally, two institutions of higher education were established in Rogers Park: Loyola University Chicago (1906) and Mundelein College (1930). Over the years, the population of Rogers Park has become increasingly diverse and aged. The 1960s saw the ushering in of Russian and Eastern Europeans while the 1970s brought African Americans and immigrants from Asia and the Americas to the region. Since then, Rogers Park has also become home to several nursing and retirement homes.[1]

## PRAY

There is a strong emphasis on church-planting in Rogers Park. Pray for unity among various churches and ministries.

As one of the most diverse and populous neighborhoods in Chicago, Rogers Park is home to many nations and peoples of different religious beliefs. Pray for missional relationships to form and for the gospel to take root in this community. Pray specifically that the numerous refugee and immigrant populations will respond favorably to a holistic gospel.

Pray for the teachers and administrators in the neighborhood schools who are serving and guiding children, among which nearly seventy different languages are spoken.

1 Mooney-Melvin, Patricia. Rogers Park. Encyclopedia of Chicago. http://www.encyclopedia.chicagohistory.org/pages/1086.html.

# ROSELAND

**JOB 24:12**

*From the city men groan and the souls of the wounded cry out.*

## NEIGHBORHOODS

Fernwood, Kensington, Lilydale, Princeton Park, Roseland, Rosemoor

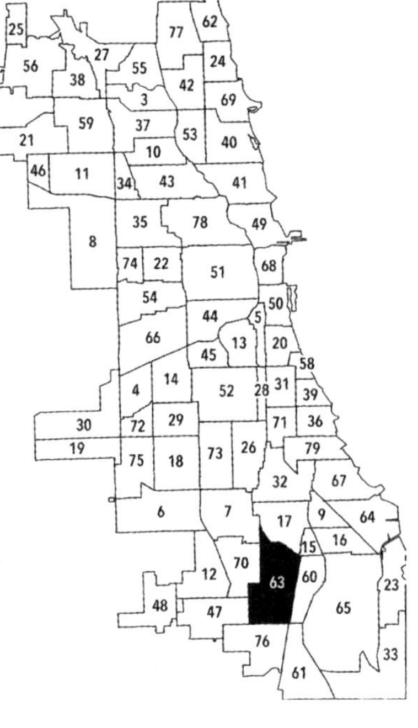


## DEMOGRAPHICS

Asian (0.1%), Black or African American (97.2%), Hispanic or Latino (0.5%), White (0.9%)

## LEARN

Roseland was settled in 1849 by Dutch farmers who were made prosperous with their close location to Chicago. The Great Depression and the end of Prohibition led to a collapse in Roseland's economy. Even more, the effort to provide housing for African Americans in Princeton Park brought greater division in Roseland, and by 1947, the residents of Roseland joined in the violence targeted toward African Americans residing in Fernwood, one of Roseland's oldest neighborhoods. Roseland is now known for its high rates of subsidized housing repossessions and has yet to recover from the effects of decades of economic decline.[1]

## PRAY

The structure of families is a rising concern for Roseland. Many families are headed by young single mothers who have little guidance on how to raise their children. Pray for programs and people who can help young adults raise their children with wisdom and nurture.

Prostitution and drugs are prevalent in areas in Roseland. Men, especially, are involved with drugs, violence, gangs, and idleness. Pray that men would seek and find help so they could be involved with and supportive in their family.

There are few recreational and other activities offered to the children in the community. Pray that they would be provided with opportunities to do things that interest them and give them the chance to learn.

There are many churches in Roseland, but few people have been introduced to having a relationship with God through Jesus Christ. Pray that the churches in the community would emphasize a relationship with the Lord instead of religious observance and for a desire in the hearts of the residents for this relationship.

1 Reiff, Janice L. Roseland. Encyclopedia of Chicago. http://www.encyclopedia.chicagohistory.org/pages/1094.html.

# SOUTH CHICAGO

**PROVERBS 24:7**

*The righteous is concerned for the rights of the poor.*

## NEIGHBORHOODS

South Chicago

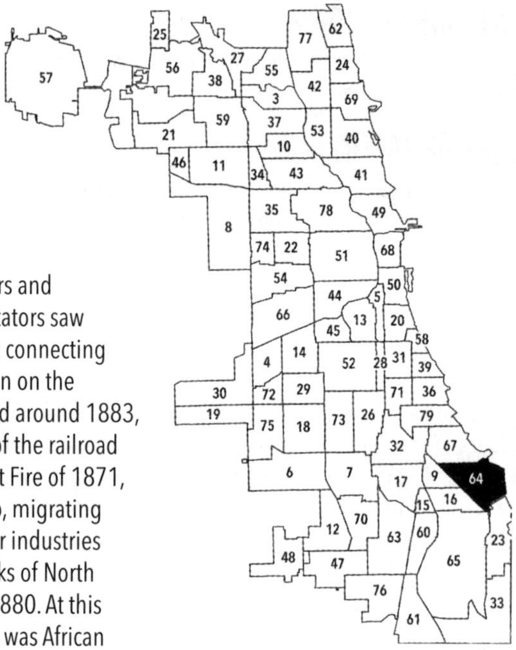

## DEMOGRAPHICS

Asian (0.1%), Black or African American (71.6%), Hispanic or Latino (25.5%), White (1.9%)

## LEARN

This neighborhood was first a settlement to farmers and fishermen, who gave it the name Ainsworth. Spectators saw promise for this area, believing it would become a connecting point for outside shipping routes due to its location on the Calumet River. Therefore, many bought up the land around 1883, many being Irish Catholics, and the convenience of the railroad also helped this area's early growth. After the Great Fire of 1871, industry began making its home in South Chicago, migrating farther south. The steel, grain, railroad, and lumber industries grew in this area as companies such as South Works of North Chicago Rolling Mill Company, which opened in 1880. At this time, almost half the population of South Chicago was African American and another forty percent Latino. In 1992, US Steel South Works was shut down, many people lost jobs, and local business was in great decline. Since then, urban planners and some industry have moved in, but progress continues to be slow.[1]

## PRAY

Although slow, there have been slow signs of economic growth. Thank God for these signs of growth around industry and transportation.

Pray for the protection of the citizens of this community.

Pray for more entry-level jobs for both younger and older community residents.

Some in South Chicago have a criminal record in their past. Pray for expungement opportunities for ex-offenders who are trying to reintegrate into society.

1 Bensman, David. South Chicago. Encyclopedia of Chicago. http://www.encyclopedia.chicagohistory.org/pages/1170.html.

# SOUTH DEERING

**GALATIANS 6:9**

*. . . let us not lose heart in doing good . . .
we shall reap if we do not grow weary.*

## NEIGHBORHOODS

South Deering

## DEMOGRAPHICS

Asian (0.1%), Black or African American (61.6%), Hispanic or Latino (30.6%), White (6.8%)

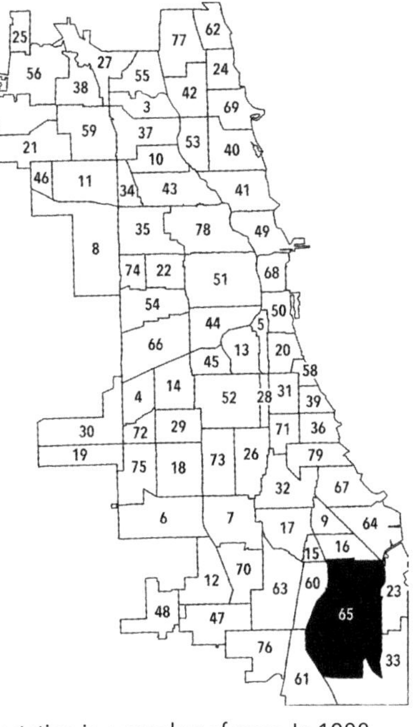


## LEARN

South Deering originally built its foundation on steel production and other industry and flourished for a number of years. However, a decade of violence was triggered in 1953 when an African American family moved into the Trumbull Park homes in South Deering. Although African Americans had been working in the factories, they worked less desirable jobs and did not reside in South Deering. Civil rights legislation brought an end to the segregation of jobs and housing, and African Americans were now able to access improved employment and housing. The next turn of events that shook South Deering was the abrupt close of Wisconsin Steel in March of 1980 due to a number of bad financial decisions. Workers lost almost all their benefits, and hundreds of residents were left jobless. People reacted to the devastation in a number of ways. In 1988, the parent company, International Harvester, settled to pay back $14.8 million of the $85 million of money from benefits, offering little satisfaction to the hundreds of families that were forced to leave, searching for new employment outside of Chicago.[1]

## PRAY

South Deering has never rebounded from the decline of the steel industry or the closing of Wisconsin Steel.

Pray for economic development in this community to supply employment to the residents of South Deering.

Pray for protection against gambling addictions in the community, as there are a number of casinos not far away.

South Deering is a diverse community, but often separated by its cultural differences. Pray that the Lord would bring unity among the residents in this community.

Many children are at risk of dropping out of school. Pray against apathy; that parents and teachers would encourage these children to stay in school and be positive role models.

1 Bensman, David. South Deering. Encyclopedia of Chicago. http://www.encyclopedia.chicagohistory.org/pages/1171.html.

# SOUTH LAWNDALE

**PROVERBS 24:7**

*The righteous is concerned for the rights of the poor.*

## NEIGHBORHOODS

Little Village (La Villita), Marshall Square, South Lawndale

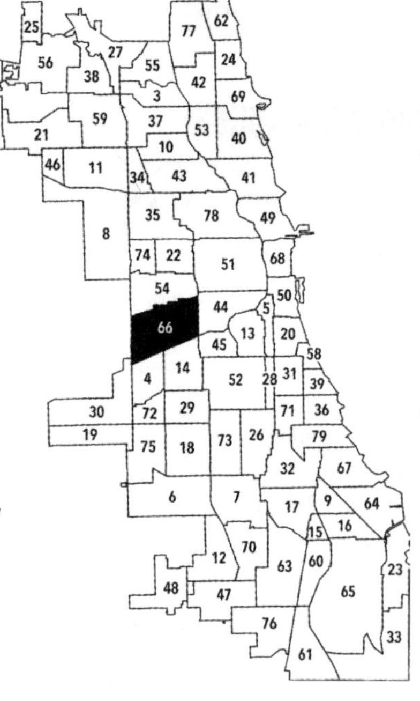


## DEMOGRAPHICS

Asian (0.1%), Black or African American (13.5%), Hispanic or Latino (82.1%), White (4.1%)

## LEARN

South Lawndale was originally settled by Germans and Czechs following the Chicago Fire of 1871. Later groups of Poles and Hispanics came in seeking employment opportunities. This working community was hit hard with economic downslides in the late 1960s. As jobs in the industrial sector disappeared, residents sought work in the service and public sectors. By 2000, 83 percent of the population was Hispanic, half of which were foreign-born. About 40 percent of the total population has been under twenty years of age; this has led to overcrowded public schools. The community also struggles with gang activity in the area.[1]

## PRAY

South Lawndale comprises a large Latino population with deep Catholic roots. South Lawndale has the largest Catholic Church in the Midwest. Pray for a clear understanding of who Jesus is.

There is strong gang violence that exists in the community, with many retaliation shootings between two defined gangs in the area. Pray for the peace, safety, and protection of the innocent. Pray for the thousands incarcerated in Cook County Jail and the ministries that are reaching out to them.

The community is home to the largest amount of youth demographic in the city. However, there are few public parks and programs geared to the youth, so many have turned to involvement in gangs. Pray for new public places to open for the youth to have Christ-centered options and activities to be involved in.

Extensive undocumented population. Pray for justice and immigration reform for families facing possible deportation.

1 Reed, Christopher R. South Lawndale. Encyclopedia of Chicago. http://www.encyclopedia.chicagohistory.org/pages/1174.html.

# SOUTH SHORE

**MARK 6:34**

*. . . He saw a great multitude and He felt compassion for them . . .*

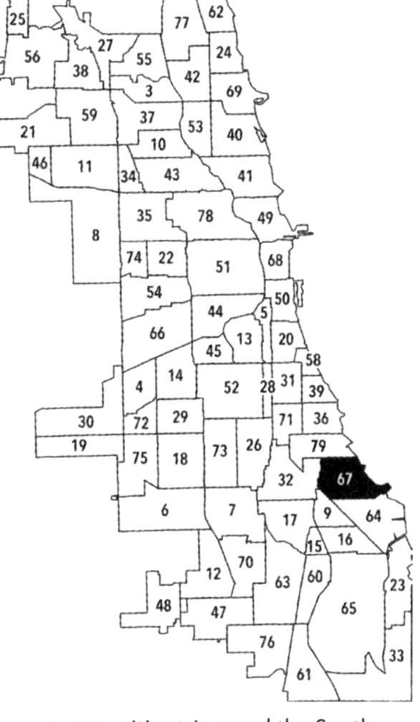


## NEIGHBORHOODS

Jackson Park Highlands, South Shore

## DEMOGRAPHICS

Asian (0.3%), Black or African American (94.8%), Hispanic or Latino (1.3%), White (1.8%)

## LEARN

South Shore has undergone repeated racial changes throughout its history. Because the World's Fair of 1893 was held in nearby Jackson Park, South Shore underwent a large housing development, in which many white residents fled the community as African Americans and immigrants migrated to the area. These former residents established Jackson Park Highlands, an exclusive residential community, and the South Shore Country Club, which at the time excluded African Americans and Jewish settlers. In the 1920s the community not only grew in population, but in diversity as well, from 31,832 to 78,755 and gained fifteen Protestant churches, four Roman Catholic churches, and four Jewish synagogues. In 1950, the fear of the instability caused by the growing integration of the White and African American communities triggered the South Shore Commission to establish "managed integration," whose purpose was to check the physical decline of the community and create racial balance, which was largely unsuccessful. Though many commercial attempts struggled in South Shore, by the late 1990s, South Shore had become a solid middle-class African American community, whose culture had been enhanced with the establishment of various cultural centers and the hard work of its residents.[1]

## PRAY

Praise the Lord for the body of Christ that is deeply impacting this community in both word and deed.

Pray for a spiritual awakening within this community to spread Christ in a culturally relevant way.

Praise God for the cultural center that provides a platform for the arts to be showcased in this community. Pray that believers would use their passions and talents well.

This neighborhood contains both resourced and underresourced groups of people. Pray that these two groups of people could learn from and reach out to each other according to their differing needs.

1 Best, Wallace. South Shore. Encyclopedia of Chicago. http://encyclopedia.chicagohistory.org/pages/1176.html.

# THE LOOP

**DANIEL 9:3**

*So I gave my attention to the Lord to seek Him by prayer . . .*

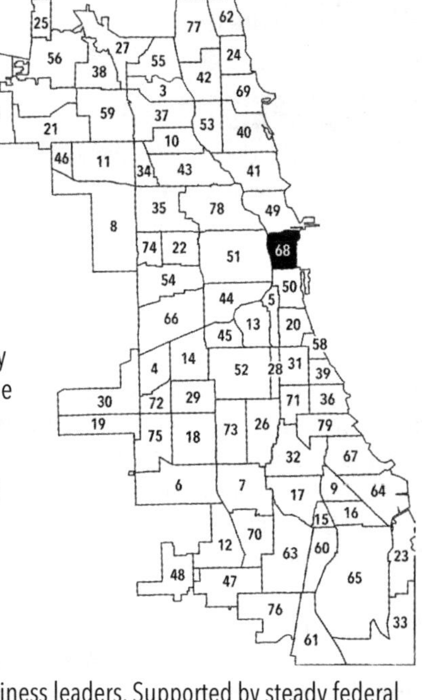


## NEIGHBORHOODS

The Loop, New Eastside, Printer's Row[1]

## DEMOGRAPHICS

Asian (12.5%), Black and African American (11.9%), Hispanic or Latino (3.9%), White (68.6%)

## LEARN

The Loop has long been known as Chicago's business district located south of the Chicago River. In the 1780s, trading posts were established on the north bank of the Chicago River, and by the 1830s, development of other businesses began to shape the Loop into what it is presently. The Fire of 1871 destroyed many residential buildings and historic churches, giving raise to the erection of skyscrapers in the late 1800s. This further reinforced the trend of commercial growth in the Loop. The completion of the elevated train system in 1897 solidified its existence and influence. However, after 1950, the pull of suburban development and the new automobile metropolis reduced the importance of the Loop. Later, the area experienced a building boom due to the efforts of then Mayor Richard J. Daley and business leaders. Supported by steady federal and state funds, the city government was able to provide offices for corporations and banks, expand facilities for educational and cultural institutions, and build hotels for visitors.[2]

## PRAY

The identity of the Loop is fueled by commercial growth and achievement. Pray that the people in the Loop would not see their worth and identity in their financial resources, but in the Lord.

Praise God for the churches and ministries building relationships, holding Bible studies, and conducting worship services at various times throughout the workweek.

The construction of multiple high-rise units has attracted thousands of new residents to the area. Pray against isolation and individualism and for residents to seek community and see their need for the Lord.

1 See "Near South Side" for more on the South Loop.

2 Danzer, Gerald A. The Loop. Encyclopedia of Chicago. http://www.encyclopedia.chicagohistory.org/pages/764.html.

# UPTOWN

**PROVERBS 31:8**

*Open your mouth . . . for the rights of all the unfortunate.*

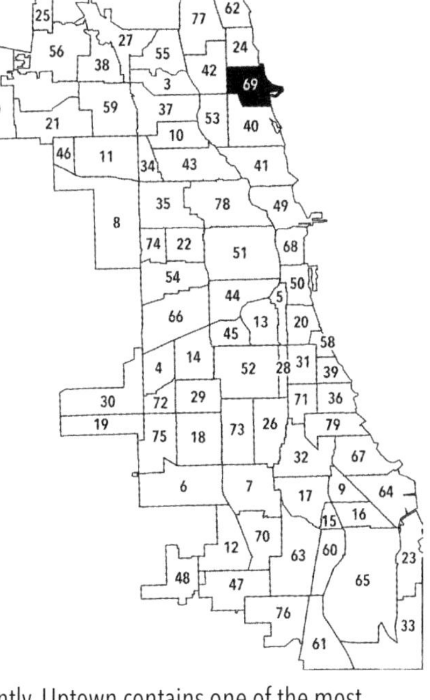


## NEIGHBORHOODS

Uptown, Buena Park, Clarendon Park, New Chinatown, Sheridan Park

## DEMOGRAPHICS

Asian (11.0%), Black or African American (18.9%), Hispanic or Latino (15.9%), White (52.1%)

## LEARN

Commercial boom in the early twentieth century established a season of affluence and glamour for Uptown; however the housing crisis of World War II led to the subdivision of luxury apartments into smaller units. These changes allowed more accessibility for immigrants and Chicago's poor. The 1950s marked a time of increased immigration as whites from Appalachia, Japanese Americans, and Native Americans began to settle in Uptown. The community continues to attract more immigrants from Central America, Asia, Africa, and the Middle East. The northern region of Uptown split off by successfully achieving recognition as Community Area 77 "Edgewater" in 1980, separating themselves from Uptown's population. Currently, Uptown contains one of the most densely populated and ethnically diverse communities within Chicago.[1]

## PRAY

Recently, Uptown has been experiencing gentrification. With the development of new stores in the region, the poor are being pushed out. Pray for greater sensitivity to the marginalized community.

There are several strategic churches, church plants, and ministries in Uptown that are engaging the community. Pray that God would use them as they preach the gospel, feed the poor, and care for the holistic needs of the people and community.

Even as the poor are driven out, there is still much homelessness that exists on the streets, primarily people with mental illness and underresourced seniors. There is also sporadic gang-related violence that occurs. Pray for sensitivity to and care for the marginalized.

Uptown is home to Truman Junior College, a university that attracts a wide array of ethnically and socio-economically diverse students. Pray for the salvation of these students, as this is a window of opportunity for the church to reach out and share the gospel.

1 Seligman, Amanda. Uptown. Encyclopedia of Chicago. http://www.encyclopedia.chicagohistory.org/pages/1293.html.

# WASHINGTON HEIGHTS

**AMOS 5:24**

*But let justice roll down like waters . . .*

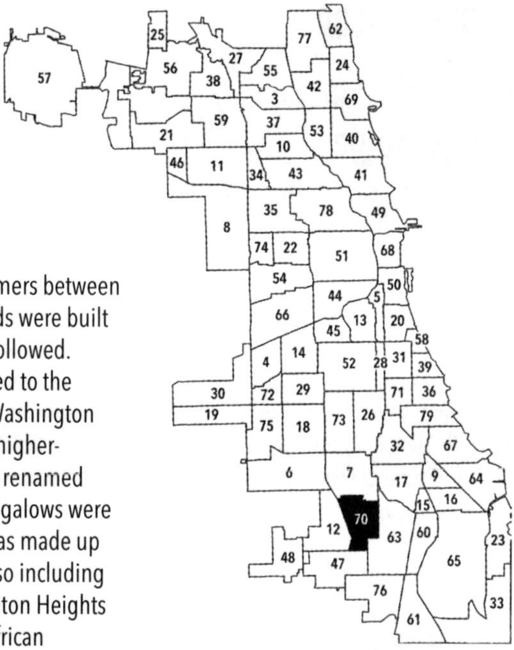

## NEIGHBORHOODS

Brainerd, Longwood Manor, Washington Heights

## DEMOGRAPHICS

Asian (0.2%), Black or African American (97.6%), Hispanic or Latino (0.4%), White (0.7%)

## LEARN

Washington Heights was populated mostly by farmers between the 1830s and the 1860s. After the 1860s, railroads were built into the region and subdivision of the land soon followed. By 1891, Washington Heights was entirely annexed to the city of Chicago. By 1900, "the heights" region of Washington Heights developed into a separate settlement for higher-income residents. This area became its own entity, renamed Beverly. Between 1920 and 1950, many brick bungalows were constructed. During this period, the community was made up of mostly white ethnic groups, mainly Irish, but also including Germans and Swedes. After World War II, Washington Heights experienced ethnic changes in its population as African Americans began to settle east of Halsted. "Blockbusting" efforts by real estate agents initiated the turnover of white-owned property to African Americans. By 1970, the population of Washington Heights was 70 percent black; by 1980, African Americans constituted 98 percent of the population. Throughout these changes, Washington Heights retained its middle-class character. Washington Heights holds the Woodson Branch of the Chicago Public Library, which has the second-largest collection of American history and literature in the Midwest.[1]

## PRAY

Praise God that this community has been home to two income, blue collar, hard-working people for decades.

Pray for adequate care for the elderly in the community, aging parents, and grandparents. Pray for sensitivity for their needs in the younger generation.

Washington Heights has been a more established community, boasting families that are long-term homeowners. Pray for continued social and economic stability.

Pray for the protection of the identity of this community to maintain strong family values.

1 Stockwell, Clinton W. Washington Heights. Encyclopedia of Chicago. http://www.encyclopedia.chicagohistory.org/pages/1318.html.

# WASHINGTON PARK

MATTHEW 6:10

*Thy kingdom come, Thy will be done, on earth as it is in heaven.*

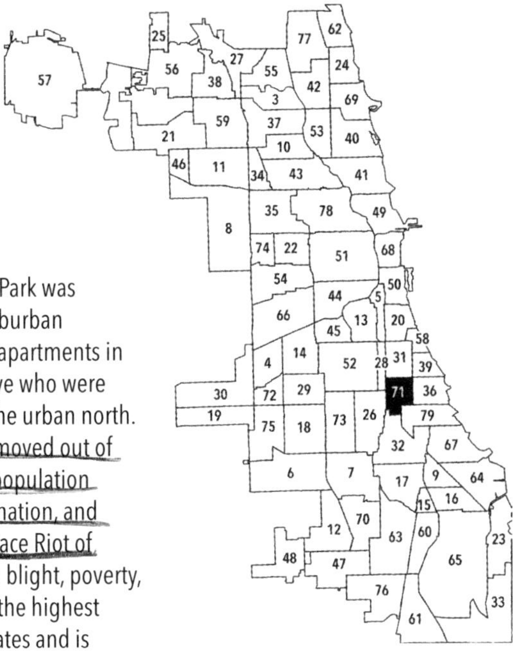

## NEIGHBORHOODS

Washington Park

## DEMOGRAPHICS

Asian (0.1%), Black or African American (98.3%), Hispanic or Latino (1.0%), White (0.2%)

## LEARN

At an early stage in its development, Washington Park was a neighborhood that exemplified diversity and suburban development. However, the rapid construction of apartments in the 1900s gave a place for African Americans to live who were moving from the southern part of the country to the urban north. During this time, many of the previous residents moved out of the area marking a drastic shift to a largely black population already in 1930. Unfortunately, violence, discrimination, and racial tension were soon to follow, including the Race Riot of 1919. Unfortunately, the area is linked with urban blight, poverty, and public housing. Washington Park had one of the highest concentrations of public housing in the United States and is significantly lacking any industry or commercial development for employment. The population of the area has declined significantly from 57,000 in 1950 to 11,717 in 2010, and nearly half of the residents in Washington Park remain below the poverty level.[1]

## PRAY

Praise God for the investments being made into the lives of young people through city-run programs that offer job training and employment opportunities.

Pray for prosperity for the residents despite limited resources within the community. Pray that families could thrive in the neighborhood and experience a sense of well-being.

There are still scars of the racial discrimination that took place originally during the Great Migration. Pray that the churches in Washington Park would be effective in engaging in dialogue to promote reconciliation and unity among the residents.

Pray for a hedge of protection for the children of Washington Park throughout the year, that they will not fall to gun violence.

1 Best, Wallace. Washington Park. Encyclopedia of Chicago. http://www.encyclopedia.chicagohistory.org/pages/1321.html.

# WEST ELSDON

**PHILIPPIANS 2:15**

*. . . prove yourselves . . . above reproach to be blameless and innocent, children of God.*

## NEIGHBORHOODS

West Elsdon

## DEMOGRAPHICS

Asian (0.7%), Black or African American (1.9%), Hispanic or Latino (75.4%), White (21.4%)

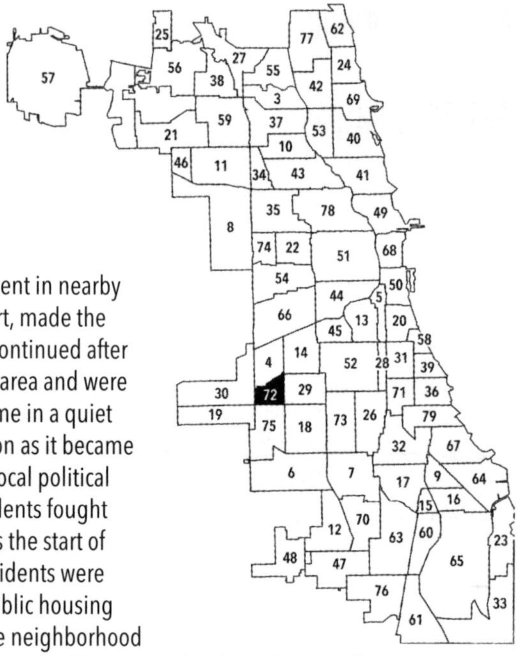

## LEARN

Development was slow in West Elsdon. Development in nearby communities' industries, including Midway Airport, made the neighborhood an attractive place to live. Growth continued after World War II as many immigrants settled into the area and were drawn to the opportunity of owning their own home in a quiet neighborhood. Drastic change came to West Elsdon as it became a strong force for racial segregation and the first vocal political opponent of the Chicago Housing Authority. Residents fought in the Airport Homes race riots in 1946, which was the start of a series of public housing riots in Chicago. The residents were successful in their riots against integration and public housing and remained a predominantly middle-class white neighborhood until the 1990s. The additional service to the Loop on the Orange Line has brought more diversity to West Elsdon, as well as suburban-style retail developments and raised property values nearby.[1]

## PRAY

There is a great need for evangelism and follow-up Bible instruction in West Elsdon. Pray for a strong, incarnational presence from the body of Christ.

Pray for the local community churches to provide the social services that are needed by the neighborhood residents.

Pray for attempts of church planting in this neighborhood to take root and connect with community residents.

There is a need for quality, affordable housing for residents in West Elsdon. Pray for the people who live in overcrowded conditions.

1 Know, Douglas. West Elsdon. Encyclopedia of Chicago. http://www.encyclopedia.chicagohistory.org/pages/1336.html.

# WEST ENGLEWOOD

**JAMES 1:27**

*This is pure and undefiled religion . . .*
*to visit orphans and widows in their distress . . .*

## NEIGHBORHOODS

West Englewood

## DEMOGRAPHICS

Asian (0.1%), Black or African American (96.4%), Hispanic or Latino (1.9%), White (0.7%)

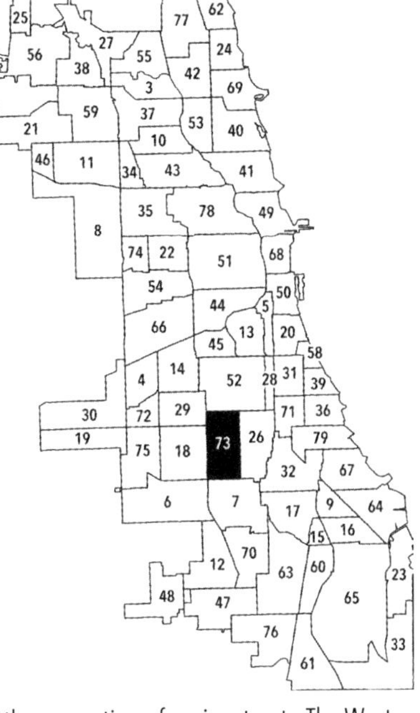


## LEARN

West Englewood's first settlers were German and Swedish farmers. By 1920, the population of West Englewood reached 56,276 with job opportunities in the stockyard and railroads, and the number continued to grow in the 1930s as African Americans moved into the area. Between 1970 and 1980, black population jumped from 48 to 98 percent. The area also experienced a drop in economic prosperity, due to the closing of the Chicago Transit Authority bus barn and the loss of stockyard and railroad jobs. For the first time, West Englewood's population began to decline. In 1990, only 14 percent of the residents had an income of $50,000 or higher and only nearly a quarter of the population graduated from high school. Many groups were established to address the needs of this community, including the demolition of abandoned buildings and the reparation of major streets. The West Englewood United Organization, established by three local churches, provided financial advice and assistance to homeowners and ran summer programs for local children.[1]

## PRAY

Praise God for the investments being made into the lives of young people through city-run programs. Praise God for the churches and ministries that have stood strongly and sacrificially against the encroachment of gangs and drugs within the community for many years. Pray for perseverance.

Pray particularly for young people in the community, most of whom are below grade level, struggling with literacy and vulnerable to gangs, drugs, and violence.

Pray for job opportunities in which employees can come alongside youth and teach them how to work and keep a job through on-site training.

This community receives extensive scrutiny due to frequent violence. Pray for the precious residents of West Englewood who know Jesus as their Savior and long for their community to experience renewal.

Pray for the mobilization of workers with the heart to plant churches, take their faith to the streets, and make disciples in this neighborhood.

1 Forts, Franklin. West Englewood. Encyclopedia of Chicago. http://www.encyclopedia.chicagohistory.org/pages/1337.html.

# WEST GARFIELD PARK

**PSALM 146:9**

*The Lord protects the strangers.*
*He supports the fatherless and the widow . . .*

## NEIGHBORHOODS

West Garfield Park

## DEMOGRAPHICS

Asian (0.2%), Black or African American (95.6%), Hispanic or Latino (1.8%), White (1.2%)

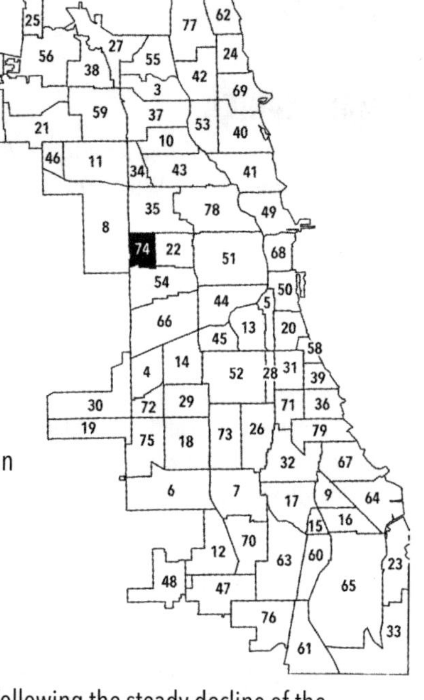


## LEARN

West Garfield Park was hit hard by the Great Depression and World War II. After the war, many residents reevaluated their commitment to West Garfield Park. The construction of the Eisenhower Expressway displaced many residents, and others feared rapid racial changes. This led to the formation of the United Property Group in an effort to stop property sales to African Americans. Their agenda was unsuccessful; middle-class black families moved to the area and formed small organizations and block clubs to protect their new neighborhood. However, these families faced overcrowding in their apartments. By the 1960s, West Garfield Park gained the reputation of a poor, disorganized community. The riots in 1965 and 1968 further damaged the area's reputation and drove the remaining businesspeople out. Following the steady decline of the neighborhood, the open-housing laws gave middle-class African Americans the opportunity to move out of West Garfield Park. Their absence left the neighborhood vulnerable to illegal drug trafficking and crime. To this day, a few organizations have remained, dedicating themselves for the benefit of the neighborhood.[1]

## PRAY

Praise the Lord for deeply incarnational and holistic ministries in this community, impacting many residents.

West Garfield Park is a community deeply affected by violence. Pray for the safety of the residents and for an atmosphere of peace to prevail.

Several school closings have heavily impacted the neighborhood. Pray that the educators would establish a productive learning environment and that the children could thrive.

Pray for church leaders and social service agencies that are reaching out to the needs of this community to have the resources they need and the endurance to continue serving the residents.

1 Grinnell, Max. West Garfield Park. Encyclopedia of Chicago. http://encyclopedia.chicagohistory.org/pages/1338.html.

# WEST LAWN

COLOSSIANS 3:12

*. . . put on a heart of compassion, kindness, humility, gentleness . . .*

## NEIGHBORHOODS

Ford City, West Lawn

## DEMOGRAPHICS

Asian (0.2%), Black or African American (3.6%), Hispanic or Latino (72.8%), White (22.1%)

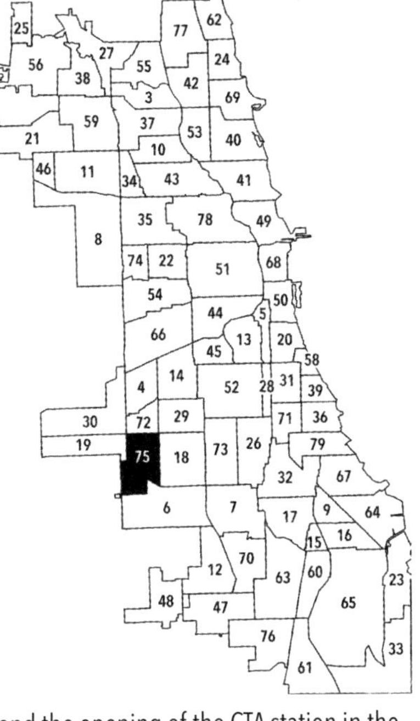


## LEARN

The population in West Lawn grew with the establishment of a street railway from West Lawn to Clearing. In 1930, single-family houses were built and the population was primarily composed of German, Irish, Czech, Polish, and Italian immigrants. The population grew rapidly in the decades following World War II. Much of the growth was due to an ethnic white movement out of neighborhoods experiencing racial change. In 1965, the Ford City Shopping Center opened on the site of a previous Ford auto factory. Other big manufacturing businesses, such as Tootsie Roll, were established near Ford City. Local retail centers and public spaces were also developed. In 1986, the West Lawn branch of Chicago Public Library opened, becoming one the busiest branches in Chicago. Renewed activity at Midway Airport and the opening of the CTA station in the neighborhood have increased property values, bringing interest into the area from parts of Chicago.[1]

## PRAY

Praise the Lord for a number of recent Spanish-speaking ministries that are serving the growing Latino community in this neighborhood.

Pray for a renewed evangelism focus on a number of Polish-speaking community residents.

Pray for a deeper level of interaction between the different groups in this community.

As the neighborhood population continues to grow, pray for a matching economic growth to provide opportunities for community residents.

1 Knox, Douglas. West Lawn. Encyclopedia of Chicago. http://www.encyclopedia.chicagohistory.org/pages/1339.html.

# WEST PULLMAN

**ISAIAH 58:6,7**

*. . . break every yoke . . . bring the homeless poor into the house . . .*

## NEIGHBORHOODS

West Pullman

## DEMOGRAPHICS

Asian (0.5%), Black or African American (94.3%), Hispanic or Latino (3.7%), White (0.9%)

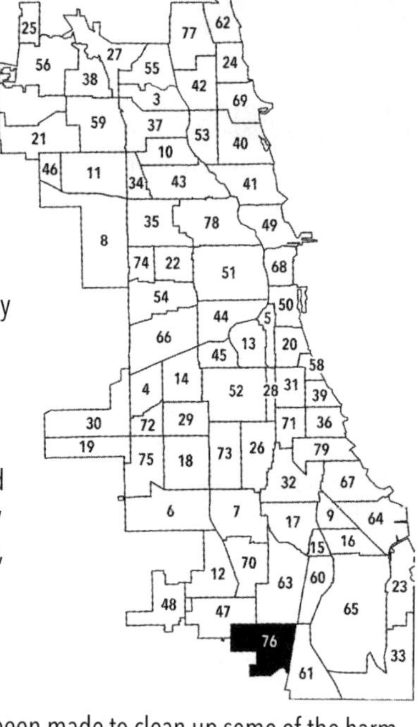

## LEARN

West Pullman had developed into a strong residential community with a large industrial base by the 1920s. The Great Depression hit the area hard, but following World War II, the area regained strength. By 1960, the population grew with convenient public transportation to the Loop and the industrial Calumet region. However, as developers started to build on once racially restricted land, West Pullman fell to predatory lenders in the 1970s, and by the 1980s, its residents lost both industrial and professional jobs, making unemployment the biggest struggle for the residents. By the 1980s, of West Pullman's 45,000 residents, 90 percent were African American. Compounding the issue of the industry shutting down is the toxic waste that was left behind, leaving much of the industrial district as an EPA brownfield. Efforts have been made to clean up some of the harm that was done, and West Pullman remains a large community area rich with economic diversity.[1]

## PRAY

Pray for the availability of jobs that can lift the many who are at or below the poverty level into a lifestyle that meets the needs of their families.

A large number of prostitutes fill the streets of West Pullman every evening, and many residents are caught in the growing influence of gangs and drugs. Pray that these people could find alternative lifestyles and Christ would be the guiding force in the lives.

Because of the many gunshot victims, there is a desperate need for a trauma center to handle these life-and-death situations. Pray for an adequate health center to meet the needs of the neighborhood.

Pray for the spiritual renewal of churches in the community to refocus their efforts to minister to families and children in the community.

1 Reiff, Janice L. West Pullman. Encyclopedia of Chicago. http://www.encyclopedia.chicagohistory.org/pages/1340.html.

# WEST RIDGE

DEUTERONOMY 14:29

*. . . the alien, the orphan and the widow . . . shall be satisfied . . .*

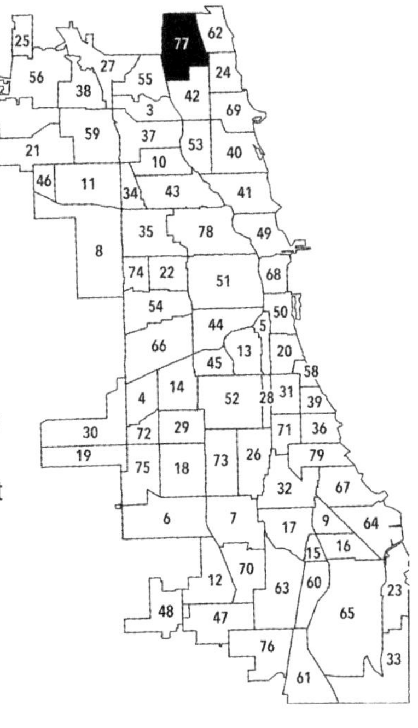


## NEIGHBORHOODS

Rosehill, West Ridge, West Rogers Park, Nortown

## DEMOGRAPHICS

Asian (20.6%), Black or African American (10.3%), Hispanic or Latino (19.0%), White (47.3%)

## LEARN

West Ridge remained relatively rural for most of the nineteenth century, not experiencing accelerated population growth until after 1920. West Ridge continued to grow steadily during the 1930s. The increasing population resulted in more housing units with the building of larger multiunit structures. After the end of World War II and a final population surge, the population of West Ridge began to level off by the 1970s. Since then, West Ridge has become a popular destination for many ethnic groups, such as Jews, Middle Easterners, Indians, Pakistanis, and Koreans. Approximately 46 percent of the current 71,942 people living in West Ridge were not native born. The area is home to Devon Avenue, also popularly known as "Little India."[1]

## PRAY

Many residents of West Ridge hold to Muslim, Hindu, and Jewish beliefs. Pray that residents from these nations would come to know Christ and that the church would see this as a missional opportunity to strategically access many of the nations who have come to Chicago.

Patterns of spiritual darkness and strongholds cling to West Ridge. There are several bookstores and propaganda that display alternative beliefs and apologetics to talk Christians out of their faith. Pray for the tearing down of these of strongholds and for Christians to stand firm in love.

Many ministries are using creative ways to reach out to the community with cross-cultural evangelism especially with tutoring children, teaching English, and showing the *Jesus* film. Praise God for these ministries, and pray for continued strength for the people serving.

1 Mooney-Melvin, Patricia. West Ridge. Encyclopedia of Chicago. http://www.encyclopedia.chicagohistory.org/pages/1341.html.

# WEST TOWN

**PSALM 55:1**

*Give ear to my prayer, O God;*
*and do not hide Thyself from my supplication.*

## NEIGHBORHOODS

East Village, Noble Square, Pulaski Park, Smith Park, Ukranian Village, West Town, Wicker Park

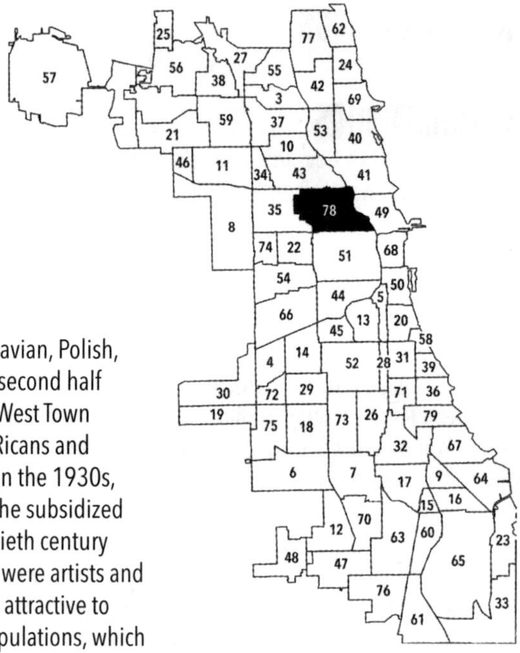

## DEMOGRAPHICS

Asian (3.6%), Black or African American (9.2%), Hispanic or Latino (30.2%), White (55.5%)

## LEARN

West Town originally comprised German, Scandinavian, Polish, Russian Jewish, and Ukrainian communities. The second half of the twentieth century marked great change as West Town became a primarily Latino "port of entry." Puerto Ricans and Mexicans moved into the area in great numbers. In the 1930s, many African Americans also began settling into the subsidized housing development. The latter part of the twentieth century brought even more African Americans, many who were artists and wealthier residents. The area became increasingly attractive to artists, students, and other young "bohemian" populations, which in turn brought more affluent residents to the area. Due to rising real-estate prices, much of the Latino community moved to seek more affordable living. West Town is often seen as the trendy and "new age" neighborhood.[1]

## PRAY

As new families move into the neighborhood, the area seems to be split into two communities. The previously settled residents are primarily African American, and the newer settlers are mostly artists and students. Pray for a unified community in West Town and against racial tension that exists.

The Wicker Park community in West Town has become especially attractive to wealthy residents and artists, whereas previous settlers have sought more affordable housing in the Ukrainian Village and West Town community of this neighborhood. Pray for the church to help navigate with wisdom and discernment in this process of gentrification.

Pray for God to reach into the hearts of the residents in West Town, who are truly diverse in their needs spiritually and physically; from homelessness to struggles with same-sex attraction, from atheism and agnostism to broken families.

1 Essig, Steve. West Town. Encyclopedia of Chicago. http://www.encyclopedia.chicagohistory.org/pages/1342.html.

# WOODLAWN

**PROVERBS 19:17**

*He who is gracious to a poor man lends to the Lord and He will repay him . . .*

## NEIGHBORHOODS

Woodlawn

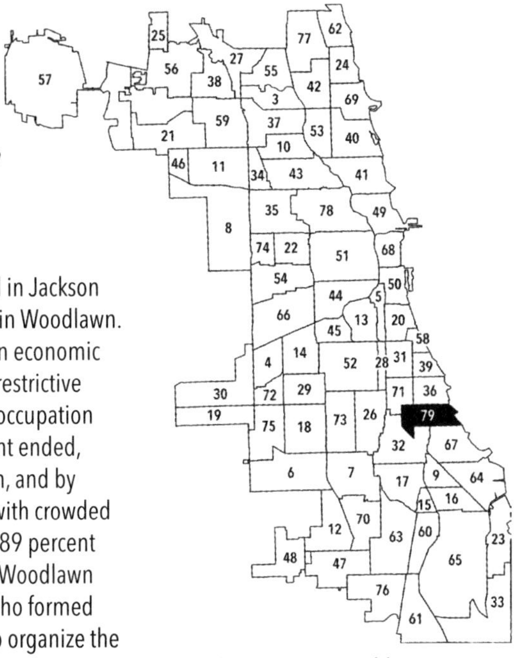

## DEMOGRAPHICS

Asian (1.0%), Black or African American (91.2%), Hispanic or Latino (1.4%), White (5.0%)

## LEARN

When the World's Columbian Exposition was held in Jackson Park in 1893, 20,000 residents made their home in Woodlawn. Likewise, when the fair closed, the area suffered an economic depression. In 1928, local land owners imposed restrictive covenants that prohibited the lease, purchase, or occupation of property to nonwhites. By the time the covenant ended, the area had declined due to the Great Depression, and by 1960, Woodlawn had experienced deterioration with crowded housing and very little economic support, and an 89 percent African American population. The western area of Woodlawn also experienced an influx of displaced persons who formed two new street gangs. In 1959, a major attempt to organize the community and fight racial oppression was made with some success, but the area was not able to recover. Residents who were able moved, especially after the destruction of a reported 362 abandoned buildings due to arson. Unemployment, poverty, and crime grew and the population declined from 81,279 in 1960 to 27,086 in 2000. However, the history of peaceful civic action has continued, and starting in the 1990s, some have attempted to bring commercial enterprises and private development to Woodlawn.[1]

## PRAY

There are some parachurch ministries in the community reaching out to urban youth, children, and families. Pray that their efforts in holistic ministry would make a deep impact in their lives.

Pray for business incubators being established in the community, that they would take root and provide much needed jobs for the residents.

Areas of Woodlawn are unsafe, especially for neighborhood children. Pray for safe passage as these kids negotiate life on the street, to and from school, and for peace in the community.

Pray for the body of Christ and local churches to reengage the community with tears, compassion, and an incarnational gospel.

1 Seligman, Amanda. Woodlawn. Encyclopedia of Chicago. http://www.encyclopedia.chicagohistory.org/pages/1378.html.

# ABOUT HEART FOR THE CITY

## SEMINARS AND CONFERENCES

Equipping churches and ministries with tools to engage in community analysis and identifying practical ways of proclaiming the gospel, locally and globally.

## BUS TOURS

Guiding participants through an experience of the rich history, culture, and diversity of Chicago neighborhoods through a biblical lens.

## URBAN PLUNGES

Providing hands-on training in urban ministry, the opportunity to experience the rich diversity of the city, and interaction with ministries God is using to advance His kingdom in Chicago.

## GLOBAL CONVERSATIONS

Developing mutual learning experiences among Christian leaders and ministry practitioners across cultures.

*Learn more about the ministry and other publications at* **www.h4tc.org**

# ABOUT THE AUTHORS

## ELIZABETH KOENIG BIOGRAPHY:

Elizabeth Koenig received her BA in social work and psychology from Greenville College in 2007. Shortly following graduation she served with Youth With A Mission in Latin America as a translator and trainer for the Foundation in Community Development School. She has also worked in the United States in resident services aiding in care-planning and transitional living in a Continuing Care Retirement Community (CCRC). Currently Elizabeth is working to receive her MA in intercultural ministry from Moody Theological Seminary and serving with Heart for the City as the project coordinator.

## DR. JOHN FUDER BIOGRAPHY:

Director of Justice and Compassion Ministries of re:source global. In 1993, after 15 years of serving in urban ministry in California, Dr. Fuder brought his passion of equipping students for effective urban ministry to Chicago. As the professor of Urban Studies at Moody Theological Seminary and Graduate School, Dr. Fuder taught ministry practitioners and students for 17 years. He holds a BRE from Prairie Bible College, an MA in Religion from Pepperdine University and a PhD from Biola University. Doc Fuder and his wife, Nellie, live in Edgewater and have three children and a granddaughter.

2705 S. Archer Ave. 2FL.
Chicago, IL 60608
docfuder@resourceglobal.org
www.h4tc.org

## OTHER PUBLICATIONS:

Fuder, John. *Neighborhood Mapping: A Basic Guide to Community Analysis.* Chicago: Moody Publishers, 2014.

*A Heart for the Community*. Gen. Ed. John Fuder. Chicago: Moody Publishers, 2009.

*A Heart for The City: Effective Ministries to the Urban Community.* Gen. Ed. John Fuder. Chicago: Moody Publishers, 1999.

*Training Students for Urban Ministry.* Eugene: Wipf & Stock, 2001.

# INDEX

# INDEX

# INDEX

# AN EXCERPT FROM

# NEIGBORHOOD MAPPING

BY

JOHN FUDER

# CONTENTS

Chapter 1

# ONE CHURCH'S SUCCESS STORY: ADAPTING TO THE GROWING LATINO COMMUNITY

Our neighborhoods are in a continual state of change. God is sending the nations to our cities and as Christ-followers embedded in local churches we are, at times, overwhelmed in how to respond. Pastor David Potete, one of my former graduate students and longtime friend and ministry comrade in the Belmont-Cragin (Bel-Cragin) neighborhood on Chicago's Northwest Side, talked to me recently about the learning curve in working with his church to engage the community. His journey serves as a blueprint for us as we study and serve our changing communities. Here is his story.

I knew the importance of understanding demographics and the need to know the community the church is trying to reach. So when I and a few others planted Northwest Community Church in Chicago in 1991, I spent $600 on a demographic study of our neighborhood. But even with that knowledge, I had no idea the stunning value exegeting our community would have on the life of our church. In 2005 as part of my graduate studies, I took Dr. Fuder's class on community analysis. While it gave me a better understanding of what it means to be a student of my community, it only paved the way to the greater firsthand knowledge that came a year later when Dr. Fuder asked me if his graduate class could partner with our church to do a community analysis of our neighborhood.

Of course, I said yes. I knew I would learn more about the area I served. I met with the graduate students, discussed the neighborhood as I understood it, and worked with the class to develop a survey. The experience was informative and enlightening, since it challenged me to articulate my perceptions in a way I had not previously been forced to.

We surveyed the neighborhood, the grad class tabulated the results, and presented a booklet with several suggestions to our church. Though I was grateful for the experience, I didn't expect some great insight that would revolutionize our church.

At the time Northwest Community Church was 85 percent Caucasian, 10 percent Latino, and 5 percent African-American. Being in the predominantly Latino neighborhood of Bel-Cragin, it was obvious to everyone that we needed to become more Spanish-speaking in our services. We made some effort, but admittedly, it was not very intentional. And not very effective. The most we usually did was to occasionally sing a song or read a Scripture in Spanish.

THOUGH WE KNEW THE DEMOGRAPHICS BY EXPERIENCE, TO SEE IT IN BLACK AND WHITE ON THE PAGE WAS CRITICAL.

When our church was presented with the community analysis report, however, we felt as if it were a smack in the face. It helped us understand our community as we never had before. It clarified where we were. And it made it crystal clear to us where we needed to go.

Even simply pointing out the demographic makeup of Bel-Cragin in the report was eye-opening. Though we knew the demographics by experience, to see it in black and white on the page was critical. The report's recommendations made it clear we must be bilingual. Community analysis gave us insights that truly revolutionized our church!

With the report and our new knowledge and understanding of our neighborhood, the first thing we did was to revisit and develop a theology of the nations for our church. We already had that kind of theology for our international missions, but it was lacking for missions around our block. We studied passages in Scripture and concluded that our mandate to make disciples starts right on our street! We now hold the conviction that we are to be a truly multiethnic, multicultural, and multilingual church. Part of that conviction is that we now hold bilingual services with Spanish and English combined in the same service.

We realized that if we wanted to serve and reach our community—as our name suggests—we had to make deliberate and intentional changes. In fact, our associate pastor, Gowdy Cannon, took the results so seriously that he traveled to Peru for a month to immerse himself in Spanish. We developed a translation team and began translating our flyers, bulletins, website, and worship slides into Spanish. We also invested in an FM transmission system to provide live translation through headphones.

Next we looked at our sanctuary's setup. The chairs faced the stage at the front of the sanctuary. One Sunday we moved the chairs into four sections with each section facing the center of the room. Instead of standing on the stage to preach, I stood in the center of the floor. When I was seated, I looked directly at my brothers and sisters worshiping. The first time I saw the joy of my Latino church family worshiping in their heart language confirmed to me that what we were doing was pleasing to God and a blessing to others. We now rearrange the chairs for this type of setup several times a year.

We still have a long way to go. Our attendance is now about 35 percent Latino, 5 percent African-American, 50 percent Caucasian, and a smattering of everything else.

There is no doubt in my mind we have become more of the church God wants us to be as a result of engaging in community analysis. And we are committed to reengaging in that type of analysis every few years to stay on track.

I thought I knew my community, and I did to a degree. However, the process of community analysis clarified, crystalized, and truly changed our approach to fulfilling the Great Commission in our neighborhood.

Armed with knowledge, understanding, and the Holy Spirit's guidance, we too can go out into our communities to meet people where they are and introduce them to the gospel. Let's get started.

## TOP TEN TIPS TO EXEGETE A CULTURE[1]

As we start unpacking exactly what neighborhood mapping, or community analysis, is and how to do it, let the following step-by-step process guide your journey. We'll go more in-depth with each of these in the following chapters.

### 1. Go as a Learner

Assume a position to understand, not judge the neighborhood. This requires humility, persistence, and the courage to push past your fears. An accepting and inquisitive posture can open doors into another culture. Linguist and missions author Betty Sue Brewster's steps of cultural learning is helpful here: Come as a learner, find ways to serve, seek to form friendships, weave God's story into their story, and bathe everything in prayer.[2]

### 2. Seek Out an "Informant"

Find an individual who is a gatekeeper, an insider, a "[person] of peace" (Luke 10:6). This is someone who will let you into his lifestyle or subculture. He is an expert who can teach you about his journey as "lived experience." She is a model (albeit imperfect!) of another belief or practice and can connect you to that world.

### 3. Build a Relationship

As much as you can, be a "participant observer"[3] in that person's life, culture, and activities. A relationship, growing into a friendship, is key because in it a "trust-bond"[4] is formed, and trust is the collateral of cross-cultural ministry. In the process, God is at work to break your heart for that community (see Matt. 9:13; Luke 13:34).

### 4. Use an Interview Guide

You may not always "stay on script," but it is helpful to work from an outline. You could apply the same categories already provided and then adapt the questions (see appendix 1) within them to meet your specific needs.

### 5. Analyze Your Data

Depending on the formality of your community analysis, you will in all likelihood end up with some form of "field notes." A crucial step, often neglected, is to examine your data for holes, patterns, or hooks. What missing pieces could your informant fill in? What interests, activities, or values are recurrent themes? Is there anything you could use to enter your informant's world more deeply?

### 6. Filter through a Biblical Worldview

What Scriptures speak to the information you are discovering? What does the Bible say about the activities, lifestyles, and beliefs you are exegeting or reading in your neighborhood? What would Jesus do, or have you do, in response to the needs? A biblical framework is your strongest platform on which to mobilize your church/ministry/school to action.

### 7. Expand into the Broader Community

Your informant can act as a "culture broker" to give you entry into the additional lifestyles and subcultures within the broader community. As you learn to "read your audience" (become "streetwise") and develop credibility in the neighborhood, you can leverage those relational contacts into greater exposure and deeper familiarity with the needs in your area.

### 8. Network Available Resources

As your awareness of the community grows, you will invariably feel overwhelmed by all there is to do, missionally speaking! You do not have to reinvent the wheel. Is anyone else working with that audience? Can you partner with another church, ministry, or agency? With whom can you share and gather resources and information?

### 9. Determine What God Is Calling You to Do

With your newly acquired knowledge about your community, what do you do now? Plant a church? Start a new ministry? Refocus your current programs? Much of your response will depend upon your personnel and resources. But you are now poised to do relevant, kingdom-building work in your community.

### 10. Continually Evaluate, Study, Explore

Our hope in Christ is firm, but everything and everyone around us is in constant motion. Is your neighborhood changing (again)? Who is God bringing to your community now? Is your church or ministry responsive to those opportunities? Are you winsome, relevant, engaging? We must always ask these questions, in every generation, in order to "serve the purpose of God" (Acts 13:36).

## Notes

1. John Fuder, *A Heart for the Community* (Chicago: Moody Publishers, 2009).
2. For more information, see Ralph Winter and Steve Hawthorne's book *Perspective on the World Christian Movement,* in which Brewster wrote a chapter.
3. James P. Spradley, *Participant Observation* (New York: Holt, Rinehart and Winston, 1980).
4. Marvin K. Mayers, *Christianity Confronts Culture: A Strateby for Cross-cultural Evangelism* (Grand Rapids: Zondervan, 1987).

# NEIGHBORHOOD MAPPING

978-0-8024-1134-1

Neighborhoods are changing as people are constantly moving in and out of our cities. Ethnic and religious diversity is all around us. Just as we share our faith, make disciples, and consistently pray, it is equally important to "exegete," or "read," our neighborhoods in order to have meaningful engagement with the people. *Neighborhood Mapping* explores the process of community analysis to help pastors, church planters, missionaries, and believers in general develop practical ways to impact the community and reach their neighbors with the gospel.

Also available as an ebook

www.MoodyPublishers.com

# A HEART FOR THE CITY

978-0-8024-9089-6

In this lively text, general editor Dr. John Fuder draws from the collective wisdom of God-centered men and women who are doing the work of ministry in the world-class city of Chicago; together they challenge us to action on behalf of our cities.

Also available as an ebook

www.MoodyPublishers.com

# A HEART FOR THE COMMUNITY

978-0-8024-1068-9

The Christian community is actively working to transform lives and restore communities throughout the city and suburbs. In *A Heart for the Community: New Models for Urban and Suburban Ministry*, you will be challenged by a collection of voices seeking community renewal. These individuals are involved in creative church planting initiatives, and they are serving the growing Hispanic and Muslim populations. Additional endeavors include serving racially changing communities, economic development strategies, and more.

Also available as an ebook

www.MoodyPublishers.com

All demongraphics taken from http://chicagohealth77.org/characteristics/demographics/

Cover design: Studio Gearbox and Erik M. Peterson
Interior design: Josh Burns and Erik M. Peterson

ISBN: 978-0-8024-1261-4

We hope you enjoy this product from Moody Publishers. Our goal is to provide high-quality, thought-provoking books and products that connect truth to your real needs and challenges. For more information on other books and products written and produced from a biblical perspective, go to www.moodypublishers.com or write to:

Moody Publishers
820 N. LaSalle Boulevard
Chicago, IL 60610

3 5 7 9 10 8 6 4 2

*Printed in the United States of America*